THE SECRET ROOM

THE SECRET ROOM

POEMS BY

JAMES LAUGHLIN

A NEW DIRECTIONS BOOK

SOME OF THESE POEMS FIRST APPEARED IN *Agenda* (London), *Agni*, *Ambit* (London), *Doubletake*, *Exquisite Corpse*, *Grand Street*, *Harvard Review*, *Interim*, *Iowa Review*, *Paris Review*, *Partisan Review*, *Parnassus*, *Poetry*, *The Threepenny Review*; in the following volumes by James Laughlin: *The Bird of Endless Time* (Copper Canyon Press, Port Townsend, WA), *The Country Road* (Zoland Books, Cambridge, MA), *The Empty Space* (Backwoods Broadsides, Ellsworth, ME), *Heart Island* (Turkey Press, Santa Barbara, CA), *The Man in the Wall* (New Directions, New York, NY), *The Music of Dreams* (Brooding Heron Press, Waldron Island, MA), *Phantoms* (Aperture Books, New York, NY); and in *Contemporary Authors Series*, vol. 22 (Gale Research, Detroit, MI).

Manufactured in the United States of America
New Directions Books are printed on acid-free paper.
First published clothbound and as New Directions
Paperbook 837 in 1997
Published simultaneously in Canada by Penguin Books
Canada Limited

Library of Congress Cataloging—in Publication Data

Laughlin, James, 1914–
    The secret room:poems/by James Laughlin.
        p.   cm.
    Includes index.
    ISBN 0–8112–1343–9 (acid-free paper).
    —ISBN 0–8112–1344–7 (pbk.
    acid-free paper)
    I. Title.
PS3523.A8245S4   1997
811'.54—dc20   96–26188
                                                              CIP

New Directions Books are published for James Laughlin
by New Directions Publishing Corporation,
80 Eighth Avenue, New York 10011

for

PAUL & HENRY

AND THEIR FAMILIES

CONTENTS

LOOKING INWARD

IN OLD AGE

The pace of time changes
And is strangely bifurcated.
Day to day it races along,
Too fast for enjoyment.
The sled is careening down the hill
Toward the big oak where it will crash.
But at night, as I lie sleepless,
Time seems hardly to move.
Each scene that passes through my head
Is almost stationary,
Often lingering longer than I can bear.

BACK THEN

It was so comfortable, so
prideful a house of bone
and blood to live in, but
now, fifty years later it's
a sack of bulging guts.
Afraid now to look in the
mirror when he's taking a
shower, loose skin hanging
all over him and more mottled
brown spots on it every day.

Hair with a natural wave
rippling back from his brow,
nearly all gone now with a
big bald spot on the top.

Nights in bordellos, parading
up and down in front of them
without a stitch on, twanging
the whangus like a drumstick
to make them twitter and laugh.

Back then it was beat them
all down the ski run, play
five sets or thirty-six
holes, but now it's don't
stand if you can sit, and
don't forget your cane.

Did he think then how good
he had it and reckon what
it would be now? And where,
he wonders, is the wisdom of
age they talk about so much?

THE ACCUMULATION

I'm looking down on them, my
children and my grandchildren,
as they struggle to get rid
of all the mess I've left
accumulated in the house. "My
god," they sigh, "couldn't
he have gotten rid of some
of these books and magazines
while he was still around to
know who would want them?"
Did he ever throw away a book
that was sent to him by some
struggling writer? The people
from the Salvation Army came
to look at them. They threw up
their hands in astonishment.
They estimated there were
fifteen hundred linear feet
of shelving full of books.
It would take ten truckloads
to cart them away and then
there would be the problem
of disposing of them. They
said the EPA had strict laws
for disposing of paper without
smoking up the atmosphere.
Where I was I couldn't give
any advice. And if I could
communicate what would I say?

I would just have to plead
I suffered from bibliomania.
A long life of bibliomania
and now no way to make
up for it.

THE HEALER

Ben Wiesel was my shrink,
a man to keep in my mind
forever. When I'd come into
his office each month for my
session he would take a
quick look at me, he could
read how I was from the way
I looked, and then he would
ask to see the poems that
I'd written since my last
visit. He'd go over them
very deliberately looking
for signs and symbols. He
read my condition from the
poems. We would only talk
about them when he came on
something that troubled him.
Then his questions would be
piercing but put with a
delicious humor and inter-
spersed with wonderful
anecdotes. He would cock
his head to one side as he
told his stories. He didn't
use any psychotropic jargon.
He didn't give me orders. He
just drew me into a mind
that was wise from twenty
years of practical teaching.

I'd leave his office walking
on air, cheerful as a butterfly.

When I came to Ben I was a
mess, in a fair way to ruining
my life. Ben put me back on
track. He's been dead now three
years, but he's still with me.
When I write a poem that I
think he would like, I mark
it "for Ben" at the side of
the page.

I'M WALKING VERY SLOWLY
TODAY

Outside and even in the house,
It's such a beautiful winter day.
I want to make it last.
It snowed in the night, there is no wind,
And the snow is clinging to every branch
Of the trees. Hundreds of tiny white branches
Reaching, but for what? Don't they know
They'll be melted and gone in a few hours?
Even now the sun has come out
With an almost violent brightness.
The snow on the trees is turning
To particles of glistening ice.
Such a shining, a cold radiance.
In a few hours the trees will be bare again,
With the snow under them roughened
Where the ice buds fell into it.

I've been walking as slowly as possible,
Outside as I go to the barn to feed the sheep
And inside as I hunt for the books
I need for something I'm writing.
The brilliance of light pours in
Through the windows. I move very slowly.
I don't want this snow-light to end.
I'd like to stretch it out endlessly.
I'm eighty and I want more such days,
But I know I'm not likely to be given them.

L'HYPERESTHÉSIE

Chaque goutte de pluie
Qui tombe dans la barrique
Devient instamment
Le sujet d'un poème.
C'est un bombardment
Impitoyable qui punit
Les sens et menace
D'annihiler la raison.

HYPERAESTHESIA

Each drop of rain
That falls into the barrel
Instantly becomes
The subject for a poem
It's a merciless bombardment
Which punishes the senses
And threatens to annihilate reason.

After Mallarmé.

HOW MAY I PERSUADE HER

To take up a few naughty ways?
She is fair as the Kyprian, the
Gray-eyed, silver-footed goddess
Of love, Aphrodite, but she, my
Passion, is so timid, so chaste.
She smiles like the divinity
And pretends that she likes me.
She flirts like Horace's darling
Lalage, but if I move near to
Touch her, if it's only to brush
The sweet little breasts under
Her tunic, she cowers as if I
Were the Minotaur. When she
Moves her delicious body it's
The graceful glide of Terpsi-
Chore, but if I pursue her
She stiffens her beauty. The
More I admire her the more
Her reticence makes me tremble
With frustration. I plead with
Her that I'm not lustful Apollo
Pursuing Daphne in the woodland.
She laughs at the comparison
And tosses her pretty curls.
I tell her that Aphrodite, who
Sprang from the foam of the sea,
Played love-games with Ares,
The god of warlike frenzy, though
She was married to Hephaestus,

12

And suffered nothing but a little
Talk at the parties on Olympus.

She becomes serious and suggests
She is not the lady in question.
How may I persuade her to take
Up just a few naughty ways?

THE FUTURE

Is the future all around us,
but we are unaware of its
intentions, ignorant of the
claims it may enforce upon
us? Was Ovid aware that he
would be exiled to a dull
town on the Black Sea?
Could Charles expect that
he would have his head
chopped off? Lincoln no
doubt feared that he would
be assassinated, but when
and how?

Speculations of this kind
tell us nothing about our
own destinies. There is no
higher power to tell us
what is going to happen.

The ancients put their
questions to oracles,
such as the one of Zeus
at Dodona and that of
Apollo at Delphi. At
Epidaurus, Asclepius
interpreted dreams. But
most of the responses of

the oracles had double
meanings.

And what of the three
fateful spinsters Clotho,
Lachesis and Atropos? Don't
bother to petition them.
They're only interested in
their spinning wheels. They
don't know or care about us.
The future will be whatever
happens.

THE GIRL IN THE MIST

One early morning in April
When I was out for a before-
Breakfast walk there was motion
At the edge of the wood and
A woman's figure came walking
Toward me through the mist.
I was so startled that anyone
Should be out at that hour
I hardly registered on who
She might be or what she
Looked like. As I stood there
She kept moving slowly toward
Me, one arm extended. She did
Not speak or look at me directly.
In a few moments she was gone,
Lost in the mist. On other
Mornings I watched for her
But she never returned.

THE MALEVOLENT SKY

The sky was always too close
over them. With the sun by day
and the stars by night it pressed
them down into the earth. It pressed
them tighter together than they
could bear. Once they had been
tender lovers, but the remorseless
sky destroyed them. The sky turned
them into walking corpses, into
shades of their former selves.

How much joy is left in life
Without the blessing of foam-
Born Aphrodite? Let me die now
That I can no longer have love
Secrets and the gifts of desire
And the pleasures of soft beds.
These were the blossomings of
Youth, giving happiness both
To young men and their lovers.
But age brings aches and bad
Smells to the man who has
Grown old. It makes evil
Flourish in his body and
Mind. It wears down the heart.
For him the warmth of sunlight
Is diminished. Children fear
Him and women despise him.
Cruel is the treatment with
Which the gods punish old age.

An imitation.

THOSE TO COME

Will those who come after us
remember who we were except for
three or four generations of
family? Will there be a child
who amuses herself by going
through cartons of old letters
in the attic? Will she draw
crayon pictures of the people
she reads about, showing what
she imagines we were like?

I'd be a fool to hope that any
of my verses would remain in
print. I must value them by
the amusement I have in composing
them. Just that, nothing more.

But what happened to make me
grow old so soon? When I was
young I never thought of old
age, of what it would be like.
And why can I recall only part
of some scene I'd like to relive
now? Where have the lost fragments
gone? As I lie wakeful in bed
what I see is a long corridor
of closed doors.

GODSPLAY

Sisupala

Sisupala was of royal blood but he had three
Eyes and four arms. His parents found this
A very frightening omen; they thought they
Had better get rid of him, expose him in the
Forest to be devoured by tigers, but as they
Left the city, a voice called to them from
The sky: "Don't be frightened. Keep the child.
The one who will kill him one day has already
Been born. Till then he will be your favorite,
Rich in fortune and fame." The mother felt better
And called out to the voice: "Who is it who will
Kill my son?" "You'll know him," the voice
Answered, "by this sign. If the boy is on the
Knees of the killer, his third eye will disappear
And two of his arms will fall off."

The king and queen set off on their travels
With many servants, and taking Sisupala, that
Was the baby's name. They visited all of the
Neighboring monarchs in their palaces. At each
Place they asked the host to take the baby on
His knees . . . but nothing happened. Not long
After their return home they were visited by
The divine prince Krishna, who was still small,
And his older brother, Balarama. They began to
Play with little Sisupala. As soon as Krishna
Had taken him upon his knees the baby's third
Eye fell away from his face and two of his
Arms vanished. The god would be the one to

Kill her son. "Promise me, O divine one,"
The mother prayed, "that if ever my son
Offends you, you will pardon him." "Even
If he offends me a hundred times, I will
Forgive him," Prince Krishna replied.

But the fate which had been predicted had
Eventually to be carried out. Many years
Later the great king Yudhishthera organized
A magnificent ceremony of sacrifice in honor
Of his coronation. All the lesser kings and
Warriors were invited to Yudhishthera's palace
For the occasion. Prince Krishna was present
And the sacrifices were dedicated to him.
But the arrogant Sisupala had the temerity
To challenge this choice. "Neither by his
Achievements nor by his lineage," he said, "is
This lord entitled to such an honor." He put
His case so cleverly that many of the guests
Agreed with him. Would they block the rites
Of sacrifice? That might lead to misfortune
For the whole kingdom.

King Yudhishthera did all he could to calm
Down Sisupala, but without success. The great
King then turned for advice to Brahma, his
Grandfather. The old man smiled and said:
"Krishna will settle the argument. What
Can a dog do against a lion? This king
Seems a lion until the real lion wakes.
All we can do is await the outcome." Sisupala
Was enraged to be compared to a dog. He threw
Insults at Brahma, but the venerable one
Remained cool. He called for silence and
Recounted the story of Sisupala and the

Predictions that were made when he was a baby.
Sisupala lost his head in his anger. He drew
His sword and threatened Brahma, hurling
Insults at him. The old man kept his dignity.
"I'm not afraid," he declared, "for we have
With us the supreme one we most venerate.
If any of you want a quick death, let him
Do battle with the dark-skinned god who
Carries in his hands the disk and the mace.
When this rash man dies he will find
Himself in the belly of the blue god."

Hearing what was said, Krishna looked
With compassion on the angry king.
But Sisupala continued his impious
Raving. Krishna told him, "The cup of
Your wickedness is now full to the brim."
As he said this the divine weapon, the
Flaming disks, rose over Krishna's head.
The cloud of fire encircled the helmet
Of Sisupala. He was split in two from
His head to his feet. The soul of the
Sinner caught fire and entered into
The body of Krishna. By the compassion
Of the god, Sisupala became one with
Him. Thus was the prophecy fulfilled.

Transcribed from a French translation of the Sanskrit.

THE ENGINES OF DESIRE

On the sixth day of creation
God saw that he was behind schedule,
He was not going to get finished
With the job on time. He consulted
His engineers and they concluded
That there would have to be some
Duplication of moving parts.
Specifically, there would not
Be time to fashion separate and
Discrete mechanisms for evacuation
And reproduction. He sent his men
Back to their drawing boards and
These functions were combined.
This decision, this poor planning,
Has led over the centuries to infinite
Amounts of dubious art and literature
Only to be described as execrable.

*"So God created man in his own image . . . male and
female he created them . . . and God said unto
them, be fruitful and multiply." Genesis 2:27–28.*

THE GREEN HAIR

My hair is turning from gray
to green. The villagers pretend
not to notice it except for a
few of the kids. The pharmacist
gave me a bottle of something
he said would recolor my hair
but it didn't work. It just
made it more green, and greasy
too. My wife has knitted a
little ski hat to cover it up,
but I have to shave extra hard
to get the green off from my
chin. I went to the Cymotrical
Institute in Hartford. They
said my condition would require
drastic treatment. They proposed
that all my old hair be pulled
out and they would implant new
hair on my scalp. They quoted
a price of five thousand dollars
for doing that. The hell with
them. I grew resigned to having
green hair. Then a friend suggested
consultation with his shrink.
The shrink, a very experienced
man, thought my trouble must be
psychosomatic. He had never
seen anything like it. After
several sessions of Freudian

therapy he reached a conclusion.
"You appear to be in good shape
physically but it's clear that
that your head wants to cease
living. Your hair is going green
because it wants to match the
green of the grass where you
are going soon. You have,
let me put it scientifically,
'graveyard hair.'" He charged
me five hundred dollars for
that wisdom. The hell with him.

LINES TO BE PUT
INTO LATIN

The lightest touch
if it is gently giv-

en can yield as much
affection as a deep

embrace   soft as a
glance swift as a

drop of rain light
as a leaf I give

you these again.

THE FEATHERED CLEFT

Why did you have to guard it
So fanatically, as if its penetration
Would bring you unbearable shame?
If you had been more generous
Both of our lives
Might have been so happy,
Two different people.

THE DARKENED ROOM

Night is a room darkened for lovers.
The sun is gone, and our daytime concerns
And distractions with it.
Now in the darkness we are close together
As lovers are meant to be.
Whether we sleep or wake
Nothing intrudes between us.
We are soothed and protected
By the darkness of our room.

"Night is a room darkened for lovers": from William Carlos
    Williams, "Complaint."

DE IUVENTUTE

When I was a young man
chasing girls I was so
hot to get into them I
never had time to learn
to savor the pleasures
of it. Fuss and rush
was all it was. And on
to the next.

Now that I'm old and
girls will have none
of me I must try to
imagine what it would
have been like with
each of them if I
had taken some pains
to learn to please them.

DO YOU KNOW

That you live in my house of dreams?
It's years since we were together;
I don't even know where you are living now
Or with whom. But such things don't matter
Because you're always waiting for me
In the house of dreams, the girl
Who when she spoke in French,
As we always did, could send a tremor
Through my whole body.

SAIS-TU

Que toujours tu habites ma maison de rêves?
Depuis des années nous ne sommes plus ensemble.
J'ignore même où maintenant tu vis
Ou avec qui. Cela ne me fait rien.
Car, vivante, tu m'attends dans la maison de rêves,
La belle qui quand autrefois tu me parlait en français,
Faisait courir un tremblement dans tout mon corps.

THE COUNTRY OF HOPE

I live in a small country of hope.
Those who want to make a success
in life choose larger, more dynamic
countries. But such places frighten
me. I haven't been to New York
in two years. Here in my rural,
hopeful, domain I can relax with no
pressure to do anything important.
Here nobody bothers me or creates
problems. I'm the village eccentric.
I have no job and I do rather odd
things if I feel like doing them.
The villagers all smile at me
in the street. I think they're
eager to see what odd thing
I'll do next. I'm a fixture.
They point me out to visitors
from other towns.

But I was speaking of hope,
my country of hope. What is it
that I'm hoping for? That
changes from day to day,
as if my hoping had something
to do with the weather. But
I can have strong hopes even
on rainy days. I should perhaps
explain that I have enough
to live on from my Social Security

checks. No problem there.
I usually lie in bed until
my hope for the day comes to me.
My hopings are pretty punctual.
They usually arrive by eight o'clock.
Then I get up to shave and make
breakfast. I don't loll in bed.
In good weather I go for a walk
in the woods. A walk is conducive
to good hoping. The exercise
helps to firm up the hope,
to fix it in place, you might say.
Then I get down to work, reading
the dictionary to acquaint myself
with new words. I'm up to
the "R"'s now. Reverist, reversement,
reversionary, revertal, revestry.
I skip all the scientific words;
they're no use to me.

Today's hope is a strong one:
that there will be a letter from
you at the post office. Are you
all right? It's been a long time.

Title from Anne Carson, The Anthropology of Water.

DOORS

(*A divertimento from* Byways)

I often find myself thinking about doors.
Open doors and closed doors. In our house
The back door is usually left open so that
Rupert, our dog, can get in or out
Without barking, or Allen, the hired man,
Can come in for a glass of water on a hot
Day, or when the UPS man comes in his
Truck with a package. But the front door
Is almost always locked. Uninvited
Visitors must ring the bell. This gives
Us time to peek out a window to see who
They are and whether we want to see them.
At night both doors are locked though
There has been no crime in our village
Within my memory, but you never know,
The way things are in this country now.

The house doors are really not very
Interesting. What's more important are
My *internal* doors: the door to my
Heart and the little trapdoor in the
Back of my brain in which poems
Come through.

My heart-door is like a revolving
Door, the kind you find at banks or
Big hotels. That door has been
Revolving steadily for nearly

Sixty years. It opened first when
Verna, the little girl who lived
Next door, pulled me into the woods
To let me play with her nipples.

Since then my heart-door has been
Almost constantly revolving. This
May sound unfeeling but I can no
Longer recall all the pretty ones,
And some not so pretty, who have
Set that door to swinging, around
And around.

Because there's usually a surviving
Scrap of paper with a poem, or part
Of a poem on it, I find it easier
To keep track of the movements of
The secret brain-door in my head.
It doesn't revolve. It's like a
Trapdoor that works up and down.
It's not very large, a mouse could
Barely get through it.

The first time it opened was when
I was about thirteen, my first year
At boarding school. The door opened
And out came a rhymed sailor's chantey,
A subject I'd copied from John Masefield,
Who was then poet laureate in England.
With pride I took it to my teacher,
Mr. Briggs. He read it quickly and
Tore it up. "Young man," he said,
"This isn't poetry, it's just verse."
The door in my brain snapped shut.

Since then the brain-door must
Have opened a hundred times.
Mr. Briggs is long dead but I can
Still see his eyes glaring at me
And hear his barked rebuke. Open
And shut, open and shut. Time
After time it's only verse. That
Little door is my guillotine.

THE CALENDAR OF FAME

"Farewell, farewell, my beloved hands"
Said Rachmaninoff on his deathbed:
And Joseph Hofmann, the great pianist,
Invented the windshield wiper
From watching his metronome.
Genius that I am, all I can do
Is hit wrong keys on my typewriter.

THE CONSOLATIONS

The delights of old age
Are the little adventures
Of the imagination.
A beautiful face recalls another
That was so much loved long ago,
And we console ourselves
Saying "I'm young again."

THE CHASM

What was it that came
between us? It was like a
hidden chasm.

We grew up in adjacent houses
in a big city. We were about the
same age and played together
every day. We rode each other's
bicycles. We shared a birthday
party each year. We didn't talk
about it, we didn't need to, but
we knew that when we grew up we
would get married.

Our excessive attachment worried
both sets of parents. They decided
we must be pried apart. When I was
thirteen I was sent to a boarding
school in Switzerland. The students
were of twenty-two nationalities,
including Prince Metternich and
the Shah of Persia, who was a
stinker. Every Saturday night his
guards took him to a whorehouse
in Geneva. His father wanted to
make a man of him. One day some
German boys tried to hang a Belgian
from a tree in the park, but he

was rescued before he died. I
had few friends but something
made me different than I had
been. I did nothing bad but
when I got home my grandfather
deplored the fact that I had
"been exposed to so much
medical knowledge."

When I came home you were much
taller, but we went to dancing
school together. That fall you
were sent to a fancy boarding
school in Virginia where riding
horses was the big deal. Your
father bought you your own
horse and you took care of it.
It was wartime and in your
school the girls had marching
drill, using sticks for guns.
You were so good at this that
they made you a captain. Next
year you were voted "head of
school" by your classmates.
You won most of the prizes
for being the best in your
lessons.

We remained friends but there
was a parting of the ways. We
were beginning to be grownups.
I went to Harvard and you went
to Mount Holyoke. You never
invited me to come to any of

your college proms. In freshman
year at Harvard I had my first
brush with "medical knowledge."

After college we didn't see
much of each other because
I was working in New York.
You were such a pretty girl,
I wasn't surprised when you
soon married a young business
man from a prominent family
in Baltimore. I received an
invitation to the wedding
but decided not to go. I
didn't want to watch you be
married to someone else. I
still felt that you belonged
to me. And sometimes I still
feel about you that way. But
there's this chasm that has
opened between us.

HERE & THERE

(*In Memory of Maria Britnieva St. Just*)

Beloved friend, you are no longer here.
They telephoned last week to say that
Without my permission, without any
Warning, you had bought a one-way ticket
For an extended journey. You are no
Longer where I had expected always to be
Able to find you. Suddenly you are
There, but where is there? Does anyone
Know where there is? Has anyone ever
Been to there and returned to inform
Us? The books on this subject are
Unintelligible. The maps to there
Are illegible. It's obvious that
There has been an inexplicable error,
An error that makes no sense for
Either one of us. Here and there
Have somehow become interchangeable.
Everyone knows that there is not here
And here is not there, but in our case
They have become one and the same place.

Yes, I declare that as far as I'm
Concerned you are still here as you
Have been for so long. I fax you this
Urgent message. Please fax me your
Confirmation that I am still there
With you, wherever there may be.

I LISTEN FOR

any little sound
even a tiny noise

that would break
the silence the

ting of a finger-
nail on a glass

the click of a
heel on the floor

even the rustle
of your dress

against your knee
any one of these

would convince me
you still exist

THE CHANTING BELL

The sound we hear is the bell
Of a buoy at the mouth of the
Harbor. Have you ever wondered
What its message for us is?
These days there are no ships
To warn in that channel. What
Is the rocking bell relentlessly
Telling us? Surely it is talk
Of death, but listen a while,
Let the sound sink in, could
It not also be an eerie love-
Song, reminding us that love
Even though it was transitory,
Abides with us into eventide.

THE COLD LAKE

That day when we went up
To Sanct Wolfgang, high
In the little mountains
Above Salzburg, the water
Was so cold we could only
Stay in it swimming about
Ten minutes. Though the
Sun was shining we came
Out shivering, our teeth
Chattering. We ran to the
Little dressing box we had
Rented. It was so tiny we
Had to stand up to make
Love to get warm.

DIE BEGEGNUNG

It was in a dark forest
Where one night I was lost
Donner und Blitz
    Erfüllung und Verlust
        Schmerzen und Wonne
            Gelächter und Tränen
I encountered a hooded figure
Who was my other self
He gave me his hand and fair words
And followed me back to this city
Where he has never left my side
    Sorge und Freude
        Einsicht und Zweifel
My other self, my constant companion.

THE EMPTY SPACE

The wise old shaman told me
that the space between our

lives and our illusions can
be a desert littered with

the dried-up bones of dead
rodents or for some of us

it may be a sargasso sea
of rotting algae don't ex-

pect that the life the
child imagines as he plays

his infantile games is the
one the gods will mete out

to him, there is an empty
space between what we think

we could be and what we are
so spake the all-knowing one

SKIING IN TAHITI

Yes you can ski in Tahiti
(you can do most anything

in dreams) the girls with
nothing on but a banyan

leaf are slaloming down
the beach in perfect form

Gauguin has set up his
easel and is sketching

furiously before the snow
melts   the name of his

famous painting that now
hangs in the D'Orsay is

Muna ta Laguna   you bet
you can ski in Tahiti.

are diseased. It's pandemic. All
that mead they've been drinking
night and day up there on Olympus.
It has sickened their bodies to
the point of putrefaction, and
turned their minds into cesspools.
They've forgotten their responsi-
bilities for us earthlings. Our
fates no longer mean anything to them.
Tell me Euparchus, my learned friend,
were they any better in chaos, when
the first of them were formed out
of the void of nothingness? I think
you once told me that when their
sickness became notable, clever
Hermes, the messenger, came down to
fetch up the great physician Hippo-
crates, hoping that he could diag-
nose and cure the divine ones.

Hippocrates examined a number of
them, male and female. He was
appalled at what he discovered.
In his Medical Aphorisms he set
down the following illnesses:
lientery, anasarca, stangury
various suppurations, phrenitis,
putrid eructations, erysipelas,
dysuria, pustules of scabies,

quartan fever, empyema, ileus,
bloody flux, sphacelus, and
other diseases which he had
never encountered before.
Euparchus, I asked, with all
these terrible plagues why are
all the gods not dead?

The gods are immortal, Euparchus
answered, how can they die when
they are immortal. Unless the
world ends they will go on tor–
menting us forever.

Is there nothing we can do to
protect ourselves from their
vindictive malice?

All I can suggest, and probably
it will do no good, is to ignore
the gods. Let's give up on the
costly sacrifices to beseech
a mercy that no longer exists.
I shall lustrate myself for
them no more.

That evening after Euparchus
had gone something began to
itch at the back of my bad
memory. Hadn't I once seen
a denigration of the gods in
the kollemata of Tantalus
of Sidon in the Palatine
Library at Heidelberg? My
memory is unreliable, but

hadn't Tantalus written
something like this?
αἱ δὲ ψυχαὶ αὐτῶν μήχαναι εἰσὶ
ἀλλήοις ἐπὶ ταῖς διαφθειρίαις ἡδοναῖς
"Their souls were only instruments
of each others' dissolute pleasures."

Hippocrates, The Aphorisms, *Books V, VI & VII.*

THE LADYBUG

A ladybug has been walking
round and around the rim of

my milk glass   she's smart,
she doesn't try to get down

into the milk where she'd
drown   she waits till I take

a drink of the milk, then
goes to the place where my

lips have left a little smear
and imbibes that   if humans

could be that intelligent.

AUTO-DA-FÉ

The irrevocable decision has
come down from the fathers
of the Holy Inquisition that
I am to burn. I'll be a fire
for the faithful to make them
even more faithful. The time
of the actual combustion will
be at the pleasure of the civil
authorities. No doubt they'll
do it on a holiday to amuse
a large crowd. I try not to
feel anger at these people
or even at the friars. I try
to believe that I'm being
punished for my own faults,
that I'm not a victim.

While waiting I'm confined
in a dungeon of the castillo
which is mostly populated
by criminals. They make a
good deal of noise but it
isn't too bad otherwise
except that my cell has no
window. But I have a pallet
to sleep on and a bucket for
excretion. The food is slop
but no worse than what they
gave us in the army when we

were fighting the Moors in
the South. Nico, the jailer
who has no shoes and the
most crossed eyes I've ever
seen is a very decent sort.
He's sorry for me. He says
he prays for me, not that
that will do any good. Now
and then he comes into
my cell to chat with me
and give me the news of
what's happening outside.
He's from Andalusia and
has some pretty good jokes.

They've given me a Bible
but the light is too bad
to read it, even if I
wanted to. Mostly I lie
on my pallet and think
about what I may have
done to get into this fix.
The decisions of the
Inquisition are never
published and my trial,
if you can call it that,
was all in Latin, which
I hardly understand,
except for some parts
of the Mass. But I
thought I heard that the
word *saevitia* (cruelty)
was spoken several times
in the friars' discourse.

Cruelty! What had I done
in my life that was so
cruel that I should die
for it in the cruelest
way to die, at the stake?
Once in the army I had
broken the nose of an
idiot corporal, but we
made up after the fight.
On the whole I'm mild-
tempered and have always
been a "do unto others"
sort of person. Where
was my cruelty?

I was puzzled until an
answer, at least a
possible answer, came to
me in a bad dream, a
nightmare that I had
every so often, always
the same, that I called
the dream of the turtle.

I'm a little boy about
eight. I'm playing in the
garden of my great
uncle's house in Cordoba.
There is motion in the
ageratum and out crawls
a little turtle. It is
only about eight inches
long. It moves very
slowly, each of its four
little feet in a separate

rhythm. When it sees me
the turtle stops moving,
pulling its head and legs
under its shell for fear
of me. The shell is so
beautiful, green and brown,
shiny, with a pattern of
black markings. A lovely
little creature. I dare to
pick it up. It doesn't try
to bite me. It's not a
snapper. Full of curiosity,
the way a child is, I try
to pull its body out of
its shell. But I can't
budge it. Then I become
angry with the little
beast. I must see what's
inside it. I go to the
toolhouse and fetch a
chisel and hammer.
Obsessively I attack
the turtle's hard shell,
breaking holes in it.
There is no blood but
there is a gray liquid
about the inner parts.
Something keeps pulsing
which must be the heart.
The head, still retracted,
seems to be attached to
the stomach.

In a frenzy which I've
never understood I

destroy the poor turtle
into a pile of sticky bits.
Then my uncle comes out
of the house and sees
what I've been doing. He
strikes me and puts me over
his knee for a hard
spanking. He sends me to
my room and tells me
there will be no supper
for me that evening. I
must reckon on what I've
done to one of God's
creatures. I have utterly
shamed myself, the most
cruel thing he has ever
seen anyone do.

The dream of the turtle.
Saevitia intolerabilis,
an offense against God.

ROSALINDA, THE DREAMER

This beautiful girl, aged 26,
was distraught; she feared
she was losing her sanity
because she couldn't tell
whether her eyes were open
or closed when she was dreaming.
Was what she was in her dreams
reality or illusion? She was
having nervous palpitations.

She came to my office because
I'm a specialist in neuro–
ophthalmology. Examination
revealed no optical disease. At
hazard, because I had never
encountered such a case,
I suggested that she glue
pennies to her upper lids
before going to bed.

A few weeks later she was back
in my office, reporting complete
recovery. "Gosh, doc," she said,
"You're a wonder. Now I always
know where I am and who I am."
Such a lovely girl; we're engaged
to be married next month.

THE UNEXPECTED VISITOR

Today, in my very own house,
there was a woman making herself
at home whom I swear I never
saw before. I'm not one to
forget a pretty face, but this
one was totally new to me.
Blonde curls in a style that
used to be the thing about
1970. No raving beauty but
nice looking, an air of
refinement. She was dressed
in slacks and a red silk
blouse. I spotted her as I
was coming downstairs to the
front hall. I could see from
there that she was stretched
out on the living room sofa,
smoking a cigarette and
reading a book.

Who could she be? I went out
to the kitchen to see if
Sandy, the maid, knew who
she was. "A lady, Mr. L. I
haven't let anyone in all
day." "Take a look please,
Sandy, to see if you recognize
her. She might be a friend of
my wife's whom you would know."

Sandy was gone several minutes.
"I don't get it, Mr. L. There's
nobody in that end of the
house. I checked all the rooms,
even the bathrooms."

I ran back to the living room.
The woman was still there on
the sofa. Was she a spook? Why
couldn't Sandy see her?
Suddenly she spoke, a
rather mellifluous voice.
"Well, here you are. I hope
you're glad to see me. Have I
aged so much you aren't
able to recognize me?"
"I don't mean to be rude but
I'm positive we've never
met." "Perhaps not in the
flesh, but I know I'm the
girl about whom you wrote
your beautiful poems 'Touching'
and 'The Enlacement.' I know
them by heart." She began
to recite "Touching" but I
stopped her. "You must know,
I'm sure," she said, "that poets
write imaginary poems, ones
to an imaginary lady like
some of the ones that the
Troubadours wrote." "I don't
believe you. Those are my
poems and you can't take
them from me." I told
her I was very flattered

that she admired my poems
but why had she come to
call on me?

We were silent for a moment.
Then she asked if I ever
wrote poems to men. She
said that the old Greek
poets wrote poems both to
women lovers and to boys,
that she had heard that
in ancient Greek there
was a special adjective
for "boy-loving" poems.

"I want you to write for
me," she said, "one of your
most passionate poems to a
remarkable young man to
whom I'm attracted. You
can do it, please write
if for me. I'm so stupid
with words. Promise me
you'll write it. I'll be
back to see you in three
weeks. I hope you can have
it ready by then."

At that, she rose from the
sofa, threw me a kiss with
her finger and disappeared.
She was gone without trace.
What am I going to write
for her, for the young man
with whom she is in love?

POETS ON STILTS

Writing on stilts is in vogue
these days. The taller the stilts
the easier to be in fashion.
Very few poets now want to walk
with their feet on the ground,
they might get their shoes wet.

These poets buy their stilts
at some beanery. Stilts from a
creative writing course are
especially prized. Such stilts
are the tallest.

Stilts can give a superior view
of almost anything the poet
wants to write about. Altitude
makes the poet feel important
and it gets him into the club.

But a word of warning to
stiltwalkers. The higher they
fall from their stilts, the
bigger the smash when they
hit the pavement.

THE TRUTH TELLER

As I was walking along the sidewalk
Of 14th Street I encountered a mad-
Woman who, without pause, was talking
To herself in a loud voice, making
Wild gestures as she went along. I
Turned around to follow her, thinking
She might have a message for me, some-
Thing I ought to know about. Perhaps
She was in her fifties, a dumpy
Little person, her hair all in
Unkempt tangles. She was wearing
A bright red dress which must have
Been given her by the Salvation
Army. Her high sneakers were filthy.

Although I got close to her, she
Was hard to understand. At times
Her voice rose to a shout. Was it
Yiddish, Polish, Italian she was
Speaking? None of those that I
Could recognize. Was she echolalic?
Probably she had been let out of
A mental hospital as harmless.
Then I got it: she was cursing
God in very rough language. "You've
Made a fucking mess out of this
Fucking world. No place for us
Poor people to live, nothing to
Eat unless we beg for it. Only

The fucking rich people have
Anything and they don't give a
Shit about us. And the fucking
Police rousting us out of the
Good begging streets, fucking
Bastards the lot of them."

That was the message, and it
It was the truth, a true message.
When we stopped for the lights
At Eighth Avenue I reached for
My wallet and gave her all the
Bills I had. She didn't thank
Me, didn't even look at me. She
Just stuffed the money into the
Neck of her dress and ran across
The avenue. still shouting and
Swearing. "Fucking world you've
Made, all shit, fucking shit."

SWAPPING MINDS

(*for Vanessa*)

Melissa and I were sitting
by the little lake in Green
Park in London playing
"swapping minds." It's an
old game that came down from
the lowlands. It was a fine
day so we had brought a
little picnic. Melissa
makes wonderful pâté, as
good as anything from Fortnum
& Mason. Yummy. And we had
a half bottle of Chardonnay
between us.

Here is how the game of
"swapping minds" goes. It's
not a child's game, it's
very intellectual, or should
I say psychological. Just
imagine Melissa and I are
talking. She says something
to me, "James why are you
always so arrogant?" But,
obviously that's not what
she is thinking. To answer
her I must try to imagine
what she *was* thinking when
she asked that. I must swap
minds with her.

I ventured the following:
"Melissa, you have the most
lovely white skin in England,
you must be careful not to
get sunburned."

Melissa: "James, why do you
pretend you are Scots when
you're really of Irish descent?"

James: "Melissa, are you
remembering the handsome
Russian boy you met in the
Hermitage on your trip to
Russia and he took you to have
an ice cream with him?"

Melissa: "James did the
other boys at school tease
you because you were so bad
at games?"

James: "Do you really love
me or are you just flirting?"

Melissa: "I'm sorry, James,
but the response is in your
mind, not in mine."

That was the end of the
"swapping game" for that
day, and such a happy day
it was, there in Green Park,
watching the ducks on the
pond.

THE SECRETS

The secrets of your body
are difficult to unlock
and difficult to solve.
I see you moving about
the house or walking in
the garden; your movements
are ordinary. But when I
watch you closely some times
I sense that certain gestures
of your body, quite apart
from what you may be saying,
are eluding my understanding.
These are rare qualities
of your physical being.

How may I define what I
observe? My feelings as I
watch you are so tenuous,
so vague. Should I even be
concerned about these strange
perceptions? Is my mind
afloat in wanderings? How
could your body's secrets
harm me? It's not as if you
had a contagious disease.

Perhaps it's I who have a
disease: a longing for
complete knowledge and

possession. Probably that's
what makes me so curious
about the secrets of your body.

THE ROAD OF DREAMS

For years I didn't pay much
attention to the things I
saw in dreams. Of course as a
child I was terrified by
nightmares, that kidnappers
were coming to get me. But
in grownup life I usually
found the happenings in my
dreams comical. I'd wake up
laughing. When later I read
some of the dreams of Freud's
patients they seemed too pat.
I wondered if the old man had
concocted them to prove his
diagnoses.

But now since old age has
engulfed me I'm having a
different kind of dream,
one that seems to be trying
to give me messages. One
persistent dream is recurrent.
I call it the road dream
because I'm always walking
on a road, one that I can't
recognize or identify where
it is. But it is serial. I
seem to be making progress
in my travel on this

road. The scenery along
the road changes from night
to night.

This dream has become like
a journey. I'm going somewhere
but I can't guess where. There
are no milestones and no signs.
Where does the road lead?
What is my destination?

A NIGHT OF RAGAS

Those all-night concerts in India
that began at dusk and went on till
nearly dawn. In the open, the audience
squatting on the ground. A platform
for the performers. The singer, usually
suggesting the melody and a soft
tabla, played with the hands, giving
the rhythm. The songs were the love
ragas of Krishna and Radha. The god
and the cow-herding girl he loved:

Let the earth of my body be mixed
with the earth my beloved walks on.
Let the fire of my body be the brightness
in the mirror that reflects his face.
Let the water of my body join the waters
of the lotus pool he bathes in.

Till I learned that the scale of Vedic
music is different than ours, sometimes I
thought a woman's voice was flat; it was
dropping eighth tones, but when I got
used to the scheme of it, the singing
became very compelling. It moved me
deeply. I can hear it still and see
the scene, the audience silent in its
appreciation of the artistry. The
shadows over the crowd lit up by
flaming lamps on the sides of the

square and over the performers'
platform.

*"Let the earth of my body . . .": Denise Levertov's
translation in* In Praise of Krishna.

Motet: AVE VERUM CORPUS

My mother could not wait to go
To Jesus. Her poor, sad life
(Though she was money-rich)
Was made for that, to go to
Waiting Jesus.

Jesus loved her that she knew,
There was no doubt about it.
Up there above, somewhere among
The twinkling stars, there was
A place of no more tears where
He was waiting for her, blood-
Stained in palms and side, he
Was waiting.

MY MIND

is drifting down the river
like a dead leaf that is
caught in the current. Now
and then it gets stuck in
an eddy. It swirls around,
but doesn't sink and goes
on down the stream. *We* know
that the river leads to the
sea, but this is not the kind
of knowledge that a floating
leaf possesses. It has no
idea of a destination, or
when it will be so wet it
will disintegrate and join
the soil of the bank.

Little leaf, shall I think
of you as Psyche or as the
mother of the muses,
Mnemosyne? In my muddled
life these were in conflict.
Often it was hard to tell
them apart. Two voices
speaking in concert.

Now that worldly memory
is leaving me, let me hymn
my thanks to both of them,
for the lifelong pleasures
they have given me.

THAT AFTERNOON

when we were walking in the sunbright woods
and you were laughing so deliciously,
"dulce ridentem" said Horace of his girl Lalage
when suddenly I did what I'd been longing to do,
pulling you to me and touching for an instant
your sweet little breast, an impulse of courage,
and of course you sprang away,
but you did not reproach me, you put your arm
around my shoulders, as if to say
you were pleased by my avowal . . .

but the god was jealous of my happiness;
you haven't come to walk with me again.

COPROPHILUS

a poet whose talent is
as small as his minus-

cule mentula has been
slandering me in the

taverns alleging that
my verses are stolen

from those of my friend
Catullus   he misses the

mark I simply ridicule
the opinions of a man

(if he is a man) who
can only ejaculate if

he has dined on his
own foul excrement.

THE SECRET ROOM

People forget (if they ever knew it)
That they hear their own voices
Not through their ears
But in their own throats.
Is there an image as well
For every breath of sound?

Yes, there's an image
But it seldom can be seen.
It moves too rapidly
And does not linger,
It escapes the eye.

Yet nothing, sound or sight
Is entirely lost—every sensation
Every face or voice
Is stored in the hidden room
At the back of the brain.
Only the keeper of dreams
Has the key to that hidden room.

THAT VERY FAMOUS POET

His rhymes splatter on the page
Like raindrops in a storm. It's
As easy as that. They require
No guiding intelligence. (Pound
Said of Petrarch that he had an
Assistant to put in the adjectives;
It didn't matter where they came
In the line.)

It's a bit more complicated for him
When it comes to whole stanzas.
But he has the answer for that too.
There a sink in his study. He
Just turns on the faucet and lets
It run till it slows to a drip.

To be sure he has to type the poems
Out or run them through his word
Processor. That can be difficult
When all he has to work with is
Squishy liquid, but he has some
Little pink sponges to soak up
The wet. No sweat. It's easy.

MY SHOELACES

(*From* Byways)

My life has been a series of untied
shoelaces. "Tie up your laces,
dear, before we go to Granny's,"
my mother says. "Granny doesn't
like untidy little boys." I didn't
do it. Granny is an old wet hen.
She spends her days lying on the
upstairs sitting room sofa, giving
orders to the servants, who are a
bunch of lazy Irish, except for
Thomas the butler who sneaks me
the Sunday funny papers, which are
forbidden at home. I read them with
Thomas in the pantry and he gives
me ginger ale.

People always warn that I'll trip
over my untied shoelaces and have
a bad fall. That only happened
once. We were in New York visiting
various relatives. I tripped and
fell right in front of the Vanderbilt
Hotel. It was a bad one. I was cut
so deep I had to be taken to the
hospital emergency room and have
stitches. This made us late getting
to Aunt Patty's lunch party at the
Vanderbilt which put her in a pet.
What I did in the hotel dining room

made her furious. It was the first
time I had ever had an oyster. It
tasted horrible and I spat it out
right on the floor. Mother took
me up to Aunt Patty's bedroom and
gave me the hairbrush. And that
was the end of the ten dollar
goldpieces that used to come from
Aunt Patty every Christmas.

I won't bore you with any more
shoelace stories, except for one.
We were in London on one of our
summer trips "to acquire cultivation"
as they called it. Mother was off
in the country visiting a school
friend, so my brother and I were
alone with father. He said he was
tired of the Burlington Hotel
dining room, he would take us to
his club. That's what he called it,
"his club." It was a house in
Bulstrode Street, nothing that
would tell you from the outside it
was anything but some family's
house. A butler let us in and took
us to the second floor in a small
elevator. We were greeted in the
sitting room by a handsome lady
who looked somewhat like the Queen.
All dressed up. She and father
seemed to be friends. They kissed.
We didn't sit down but the queen
lady went out and came back with
the most beautiful girl I had

ever seen. "This is Winifred," the
Queen said, "she'll entertain you
young men for half an hour." Then
she and father went off somewhere.
Winifred was a princess for sure,
she was wearing a rather scanty
dress but it was made of gold.
This was many years ago but
I can still see how lovely she was.
And she was nice. "What will it be,
gentlemen," she asked, "chess or
checkers?" Neither of us had ever
heard of chess, so we said checkers.
As she was going to get the checkers
set she noticed my untied shoelace.
"Dear me," she said, "your man doesn't
take very good care of you, does he?"
And, if you'll believe it (I still
can't) this gorgeous princess knelt
right down on the floor beside me
and did up not one, but redid both
of my laces. Then we played checkers
and the butler brought us ginger
and bitters, as he called it. I
suppose I should have been embarrassed,
but I wasn't. I'll never forget her
or our visit to the house in
Bulstrode Street.

THE LOVE PUDDLE

is not deep but it's
usually muddy. If you

stray into it you won't
drown but you may come

out of it looking like
a tramp and with your

feelings more dishevel-
led than your trousers.

You may feel guilty or
feel betrayed or even

disgusted, you'll wonder
why you walked through

the love puddle instead
of going around it. But

you know you'll do it
again—that's for sure.

MOMENTS IN SPACE

No exact moment is recorded for
When I left time and entered
Space; nothing precise that I
Could put down in my diary. The
Journalists were vague about it,
Using condolent euphemisms that
Weren't believed (there had been
So many cries of "wolf"). The lady
Judge at the probate court was
Annoyed. "I *must* have a date,"
She said. It was gradual, not
What I'd anticipated. It reminded
Me of dirty water running out
Of a bathtub with a little swirl
And a sucking sound when it was
All empty. Of course everyone
In the village knew something
Was happening. I would meet them
In the pharmacy or at the post
Office and not remember the
Names of people I'd known for
Fifty years. I think they'll
Miss me; I gave them a lot of
Laughs, the village eccentric.

It's too soon to give much of
A report on space. I'm just
Beginning to get my bearings.
No asteroids or astronauts in

Their capsules so far. No trees
Or grass but beautiful cloud
Formations. It's a relief not
To have to bother with eating.
Few people around and none
I'd met in books. (I'd like
To see Godot again.) But space
Is endless   it streches out
To nowhere. I may easily be
A million light years away.

LOVE IS THE WORD

Love is the word he hopes
that she will utter at
dusk as they have been sitting
on the bank of the river,
watching the dark fall and
quietly talking, but not
about themselves.

Love is the word he would
so much like to hear.

Gently, he takes her hand
but there is no response
to the pressure of his
fingers. While there is
light enough, they watch
the eddies in the water.

Love is the word he would
so much like to hear.

What should he say to
make her speak it? They
have been keeping company
for several months, but
they are both so shy. He
has no experience with
wooing other girls. She
never talks about such

things. He has no inkling
of whether she has had a
lover.

Love is the word he would
so much like to hear.

When it's full dark they
can no longer see the eddies
in the water but they hear
the various sounds that the
river makes as it follows
its course to the sea.
Then there is a brightening
in the air over the forest
across the stream and a moon,
a nearly full moon, appears.
He wants to linger but she
looks at her wristwatch and
says: "My goodness, it's
after nine, I must go home."
She rises abruptly and starts
walking to where they have
left the car on the highway.
He tries to take her arm to
guide her through the trees,
but she says: "Don't worry
about me, I know the way, I
can see it in the moonlight."

Love is the word he would so
much have liked to hear.

THE LANGUAGE
OF MY MIND

I've been trying to read
the language of my mind.
I'd like to be able to
write the kind of poem
that Gary writes, but
it's hard to do, hard
to get his concrete
simplicity and his
intonation.

I study the language
that's in my mind but
it gets confused because
words start turning into
pictures. My eye is so
visual.

So many mountains and
rivers. Kanchenjunga
at Darjeeling. The
Ganges at Benares. One
after another my page
fills up with scenes
and people.

Ezra on the beach at
the Lido. The big
glacier above Zermatt.

Sri Nalanda expounding
Vedanta at Trivandrum.

I cover my eyes to blot
out the kaleidoscope of
scenes. That's better.
The words begin to come
back. Now I recite the
mantra *om mani padme
hum.* That's not my
language but I'll try
to make it mine. I'll
say it's the jewel
at the heart of the lotus.

LUCINDA

It's not hard to write love
poems to Lucinda because we've
never met, I've never set eyes
on her. She answers my letters
in a pretty girlish hand, but
when I request a photo it never
comes. I tell her I don't care
if she has three Picasso eyes,
I know how perfect her soul is
from other evidence.

It all began when she sent me
her stories to publish at New
Directions: exquisite, subtle,
sensitive stories that bowled
me over. A girl who could write
such stories could only be the
one I'd been dreaming of ever
since I became a publisher.

I actually know more about
her than you might suspect.
For me she is Catullus' Lesbia
and Tibullus' Delia, she's
Herrick's Julia, Rochester's
Phillis. Four yummy girls
anthologized into one. What
more could any publisher desire?

THE LOGODAEDALIST

I am Bosco, the logodaedalist.
It's my job to repair broken-down words,
To make old, sick words sound new,
And make some of them seem like
    two words instead of just one.
Gertrude Stein worked at this trade
But she wasn't always too good at it.
I think she didn't always understand
That no matter how sick a word was
It still had to mean something,
Almost anything would do but something.
In the end she gave up trying.
But I'm only eighty and I intend
    to keep trying.
I'm Bosco, the obsessed logodaedalist.
As long as there are any loose words around
I'll try to make them hop, skip and jump
    for you,
And maybe make them say something
You didn't know they meant.

THE LONG MOMENT

(*for Elizabeth Lund*)

It was October and the woods
where they walked that afternoon
were ablaze with red and orange
color. Down at the lake there
was a heron standing motionless
on one leg. What was he doing
here so late in the year?

When they got back to the house
she made tea and they sat for
an hour talking about the poets
they loved. She was so pretty
and so bright. And she had a
sense of humor.

When it came time for her to
drive back to Boston, he went
out to open her car door for
her. But he didn't close the
door at once. There was some-
thing he would have said to
her if he dared.

She didn't start her car right
away. Did she have something
to say to him, too, but didn't
know how to put it?

There was a long silent moment
between them as they looked at
each other. But it became an
almost ludicrous moment. Then
they shook hands very formally,
and she drove away.

THE LONGEST JOURNEY

As a young man, full of eagerness,
I set out to conquer my little
sphere. If it were only a finger's
width, it would be mine, all mine.
And I walked, as the old poet said,
"multas per gentes et multa per aequora"
in pursuit of the voices that called me.
And some were where I expected
to find them and some were not.
And as I drew near to them many
faded away and were no longer audible.
Now, in old age I think back to those
I loved rather than to anything
I took from anyone for my enrichment,
for I know now that "the beauty is in
the walking; we are destroyed
by destinations."

"multas per gentes et multa per aequora": *Catullus CI.*
"the beauty is in the walking. . . .": *attributed to*
 Gwyn Thomas.

LONGING & GUILT

(for Vanessa)

It's past midnight but he
Can't sleep. He thrashes
In bed, probing his memory
For answers that may never
Come. He longs for her, how
He longs for her; he would
Like to be encompassing her
With his love. But she is
Far away, perhaps never to
Be regained. How much of
The distance that is now
Between them came about
Because he never learned
To love her in the way she
Needed to be loved. Guilt
And longing together are a
Terrifying torment. It's
No wonder he can't sleep.

THE BLACK HOLES

that the astronomers have
discovered are up in the
astral galaxies. They are
immeasurably distant, far
away beyond calculation.
But I know of one that is
very near at hand. It's
called anima (the soul)
and it's inside my body,
linked to my heart and my
brain by a cord of electrons.
Its blackness and depth,
which I'll never be able
to penetrate, are the locus
of doubt, of the ultimate
unanswerable questions:
who am I and what are all
of us doing on this earth?

AKHMATOVA'S MUSE

She comes to the poet only
Late at night, when the
Poet is sleepless, waiting
For her visit. Life is so
Uncertain. Is the muse a
Living person or a shade?
It's impossible to discern
In the darkness if she is
Old or young. Well, what
Matters it when without the
Muse there would be no song.

Now the muse has come at
Last; it's nearly dawn.
But tonight she stares at
The poet as if she doesn't
Know her. It's frightening.
The poet must put her to
The test. She asks the muse
Whether it was she who
Guided Dante on his journey
Through Hell. The muse is
Silent for a moment as if
She can't remember. At last,
Very quietly, she answers,
"Yes it was I who led him
Through the circles of Hell."

who lives in my flower
garden never seems to
know where he wants to go.
He zigzags through the
plants with no obvious
destination. Now and then
he'll retract his head
under his carapace as if he
wanted to get his bearings,
but soon his head will pop
out and he'll be on his
way again, plodding along ever
so slowly, one leg after
another. Does he take
note of me? Is he afraid
of me? From the deliberation
of his movements I can't
tell. I like him, he does
no harm. He's not one of
those snappers that are
over in the marsh. I enjoy
watching him and like to
work in the garden when
he's there. I've often
wanted to follow him to
see where he goes and find
out what he eats. But he's
so slow it would take hours
to pursue him. I have an

affinity with my turtle.
Like him I'm a slow mover
now that I'm old. There's
something between us but
I can't define what it is.
He is my friend the turtle.
Am I to him a friend?
Does he know what a man
is? Am I his man? I hope so.
You can't have enough
good friends.

AN AMOROUS DIALOGUE

The first time I saw her I trembled
At her beauty. But the second time
There was mockery, even hostility
In her tone. On our next meeting,
To defend myself, I used lines from
Martial, one of his nasty bits:
Os et labra tibi lingit, catellus;
Non miror, merdas si libet esse
Cani (which means: your little dog
Licks your face and lips: I'm not
Surprised, I knew dogs like to eat
Shit). To my surprise she understood
What I had said and replied from
The same poet: ventris onus misero,
Nec te pudet, excipis auro (aren't
You ashamed to deposit your load
In a golden bowl, you show-off?).
"You are a crude vain pig," she
Told me, "but at least you have
Something between your ears."

After that we met now and then
In various romantic locations
Along the banks of the Isar in
Munich. There were little word
Swords from both sides. But
When we'd exhausted each others'
Shafts there were no amorous
Sequels to our conversations.

She demurred at being kissed
And even refused to hold hands
As we strolled through the
English Gardens. It was back
To the beginning. I trembled
At her beauty and she called
Me "Schweinlichkins." I'd like
To know what has become of her.
Whom is she tormenting now?

Martial: 1, xxxiii and 1, xxxvii.

THE APSARASES

I think someone is watching
Me. Someone is following me,
I'm sure, but is not visible.
How do I know I'm being
Followed? There are little
Sounds of someone walking
Behind me, sounds as soft
As the flutter of a bird's
Wings, but when I turn around
There is no one there. And
Sometimes if I wake up in
The night I sense there is
Someone in the darkness. One
Day I walked on the beach
And there were strange marks
On the sand but they weren't
Like footprints. I suppose
I should be frightened but
I'm not.

In the puranas of Hindu
Mythology we may read of
The apsarases, sacred nymphs,
Who can make themselves
Invisible, and who can fly
Great distances, even over
The oceans. One of their
Roles is to protect and
Guide persons whom the gods
Have chosen to find dhamma-
Pada, the true way, the
Path to virtue and wisdom.

THE ACROBATIC DANCERS

(for Anne Scoville)

The two dancers, one a woman
and the other a man, who are performing
on the stage of a theatre, are,
to tell the truth about them,
lost. They are completely lost.
This, of course is not known
to the audience, which gives
them thunderous applause as
they take their bows.

But they are lost in the world
and to each other. As they sit
on the bench backstage, getting
their breath after the exertion
of dancing, she asks him, "Who
are you anyway, I don't know you."

"I think my name is Hippias," he
answers, "but I'm not quite sure.
For that matter, who are you?
Have I seen you before?"

"Probably not," she says, "I'm
from Ionia. There they called
me Nerissa after my mother."
When they had changed in
their dressing rooms they met
again at the stage door of
the theatre.

There were more questions.
"Where are we supposed to go
now?" "I don't know. My
control is Terpsichore, but she
hasn't sent me any word
of instruction." "I'm in
the same boat. My man is
Apollo but he's always
out chasing maenads in the
woods or getting drunk up
on Olympus. Not a word from
him all week."

"Well Hippias," Nerissa
says, "the gods are idiotic,
but we'll have to eat till
we hear from them. Isn't
that a McDonald's down the
street? Let's go there and
hope for the best."

*Note: The poet despairs of answering the dancers' questions.
He hopes that his friend the sculptress can do better using visual
methods.*

ALL THE CLOCKS

in the house have stopped running.
They've quit moving their hands
at different times. It's very confusing.
The kitchen clock stopped at 6:35.
The grandfather clock, that has to be
wound with a key, gave up at 10:15,
and the key won't turn in it now.
The alarm clock by my bed is mute
at 4:30. How did I manage when I was
a child and couldn't tell time?
I went by light and dark. And whether
I was hungry. That will have to
do me till the clocks end
their strike. Or will the strike
spread to other houses? I must
call up the neighbors to see
whether their clocks have given
up too and what they are doing
about it. This situation is a
nuisance but, honestly, I don't
really blame the clocks. Can you
imagine what it's been like for
them? Minutes, hours, days, weeks,
months, years plodding around
the same circular treadmills,
being taken for granted, no thanks
to them from anybody. This could
stop the world. If we get out of
this somehow and history goes
on, will historians write about
the revolution of the clocks?

ALONG THE MEADOW STREAM

The fluffy grasses on the edges
Of the stream hide my drifting line
And fly from the trout. Over the years
A deal of dreaming has drowned
In the limpid water. "Your mooning
Makes no knowledge," my grandfather
Used to tell me. "Let the fish be.
Get back to your books, lazy boy."
His voice has gone two lives away;
It stirs the water no longer along
The banks of the meadow stream.

HIS PROBLEM

Was an excessive interest
In the life of language.
There was no place for the
Emotions in his existence.
He was passionately absorbed
In words, as much with words
Themselves as with what they
Were saying. More and more,
The words built a wall around him,
Shutting him off from those
He should have loved and
Those who wanted to love him.

WHERE IS THE COUNTRY

We were always searching for,
That happy country we read about
In books when we were young?
Once we thought we'd found it,
And for a time we visited there,
But then we knew we'd been deceived;
It was not the dreamed-of country.
Or had we just deceived ourselves?
In making the choice of each other
Had we destroyed the happy land?

NOW AND THEN

He falls asleep a lot,
Only cat naps but it's rude
And embarrassing when there's company.
He's sitting in his stuffed chair,
More or less attentive to the conversation,
Then suddenly he drops off.
"Where have you been, Gramps?"
His granddaughter asks him.
"Just on a trip," he tells her.
"Now and then I like
To take a little trip."

THE NEW YOUNG
DOCTOR

at the clinic is fresh
out of medical school
and hospital internship.
He's up to date on all
the new cures he reads
about in the journals.
Some of the old fogies
here in the village
won't go to him, but
I think he's great. At
my last check-up he
told me I'd probably
live to be a hundred
because I have such a
good pulse in my feet.

A WINTER'S NIGHT

The outside, where the snow
Is softly and soundlessly
Falling (there is no wind
Tonight) has brought its quiet
Into the house that was noisy
All day with TV voices,
The telephone ringing,
And the happy shouts of children
Romping from room to room.
Now, except for me, sleep
Has taken over the house.
I bring the silence of the dark
Outside into it. I wrap that
Around my cares. Soon I too
Will be sleeping.

THE DAZE OF LOVE

Comes sometimes from
the blaze of light
when an asteroid
passes us too near.

There is also
the softer radiance
when we are separated
and sink into sleep
thinking of each other.

THE TRANSIENTS

She told me there had only
been three great loves in her life
but there were quite a few
transients, as she called them.
Don't misunderstand me, she said,
I've never been wild,
but you know how it is,
when you're young and going out
quite a bit, exploring life,
when a man gets insistent,
a nice enough man you like a little,
it's just too tiring to say no
because it means making a scene.

OPHELIA

She wanders in the meadow
Picking posies; she wanders
Among the willows singing
Sad little songs that have meaning
Only for her. She falls (or walks)
Into the stream, but she doesn't
Struggle in the water because
She imagines she's flying
up into the clouds, high up
Where there are no more troubles.

JACK JIGGER

They call me Jack Jigger because
I'm entirely made of little pieces
Taken from other people (some are
Alive, some dead). If there were
An autopsy the coroner would have
A hard time identifying which bits
I was born with, which were really
Mine. I can hear him saying to his
Assistant: "There's a lot of foreign
Stuff in here, things I never ran
Across before." When I walk fast
I hear a kind of rubbing inside,
Like bits of paper rustling. That's
How it is, pieces of paper moving
Against each other. The doctor has
Tried every kind of coagulant.
But no use. He's given up on me.

MANY LOVES

She changes the way
she does her hair for
each new admirer. If
she is to have many
loves she wants to be
a different person
for each one of them.

THE BIRD OF ENDLESS TIME

Your fingers touch me like a bird's wing
like the feathers of the bird that returns

every hundred years to brush against a
peak in the Himalayas and not until the

rock's been worn away will time and the
kalpas end   why do I think of the fable

when I'm close with you   merely because
I want so many lives to feel your touch.

KALPA: *in Hinduism, an eon, a vast period of time that encompasses
the creation and dissolution of a universe.*

SWEET CHILDHOOD

Why can't we pretend that
We're children who are
Playing with each other,
Not really understanding
What we're doing, but it's fun
It feels good and there is
An urgent curiosity to study
Each other's parts. Sweet childhood,
Happy time of innocence, come back
For us, bring back an hour
When everything was gentle and new.

SATURN

Many among the ancients believed
that Saturn was the bringer of
old age and death. But be of
good comfort. The true mythology
sets forth that as a god he was
benevolent, the founder of
agriculture at Rome, where his
reign was called the age of
gold. His *saturnalia* celebrated
the growing of crops and was
a period of general festivity.

EPIGRAMS AND COMIC
VERSES

SOME PEOPLE THINK

that poetry should be a-
dorned or complicated   I'm

not so sure   I think I'll
take the simple statement

in plain speech compress-
ed to brevity   I think that

will do all I want to do.

IN THE HIGHSTREET
OF TRALEE

Run girl, run!
Under your blue blouse
The birdie paps are flying.

God made you thus
To pleasure us
Against our dying.

THE VOYEUR

Pull up your skirt
just an inch or two

above your knees
sit quietly where

I may watch you
from across the

room   I am old and
impotent but such

small pleasures can
still give me delight.

PASSPORT SIZE WILL DO

I beg you to send me your picture
For my album of imaginary conquests
You will be in excellent company
I am not (even in my imagination)
Promiscuous and invite only the best.

AT THE POST OFFICE

It makes his day when
by happy chance he en-

counters her on his morn-
ing visit to the post office

it's as if a rose had
opened to greet him.

HEART ISLAND

Stop searching stop weeping
she has gone to Heart Island

where the Truth People live
eating fern-shoots & berries

where there is no fighting
no sin no greed no sorrow

FOR THE FINDERS WITHIN

I cannot name them nor
tell from whence they

come   I cannot summon
them nor make them lin-

ger   they come when they
wish (and when least ex-

pected) and in a moment
they are gone leaving

their burst of words
which become my song.

CARROTS

Little girls in France, even
in the best families, are told
that if they eat their carrots
they'll grow up with pink thighs.

THE HAPPY POETS

What's happiness?
It's to lie side
By side in bed
Helping each other
Improve our poems.

THE TWO OF THEM

One kept his stomach full.
The other nourished his imagination.
It was a perfect arrangement
Until some confusion arose
As to which one should do which.

THE GIFT

In that parking
lot pressure of

your body against
mine   iteration of

the dream of love

IN SCANDINAVIA

at country dances the
girls tuck the boys'

handkerchiefs in their
armpits and give them

back to be sniffed.

YOU'RE TROUBLE

aren't you asked the pretty
lady with whom I'd been con-

versing at the dinner party
I was trouble I told her when

I was young lots of trouble
but now I'm old and harmless.

THE OLD MAN'S LAMENT

He says that when the posthos
don't work no more it's like

the pain an amputee feels in
the foot that's been cut off.

DANS L'ATTENTE

Avec patience j'attends
Le jour où tu découvriras
Que c'était toujours
Moi que tu attendais.

WAITING

Patiently I'm waiting
For the day when you'll discover
That it was always me
You were waiting for.

I SUPPOSE

the rhetoricians might call this
a variety of the pathetic fallacy

but when we talk on the telephone
I imagine I hear cunt in your voice

the soft slish of honey on silk as
Henry Miller used to describe it.

ELUSIVE TIME

In love it may be dangerous
to reckon on time to count

on it   time's here and then
it's gone   I'm not thinking

of death or disaster but of
the slippage the unpredictable

disappearance of days on which
we were depending for happiness.

DEATH LURCHES TOWARD ME

but the gods do have
some pity   in these

last months the verses
seem a bit less paltry

not quite so garrulous
touches of truth in them.

BETTER THAN POTIONS

Our village love counsellor
tells her lovelorn young

clients that kittens cannot
be caught but if you stay

where you are and do some-
thing interesting the kit-

ten will soon come to you.

A VISIT TO PARIS

Why not, asked my French
friend, have your red

ribbon of the Légion
sewed to your pyjamas?

THIRTY-NINE PENTASTICHS

A Note on the Form

A "pentastich" refers simply to a poem of five lines, without regard to metrics. The word is Greek derived, from *pentastichos,* though few examples survive from ancient times. In the *Greek Anthology,* there are some anonymous five-line epigrams, as well as one each by Empedocles, Palladas, Palladius, and (perhaps) the Emperor Constantine. Some other, later examples of five-line poems can be found in French, Italian, Spanish, and Chinese poetry. In English, the best-known five-liner is, of course, the popular limerick, though Tennyson and Poe used rhyming forms of five-line continuous stanzas. The most developed pentastich is the classic Japanese *tanka,* in lines of 5, 7, 5, 7, 7 syllables. The *tanka* influenced the American poet Adelaide Crapsey (1878–1914), whose posthumously published unrhymed "cinquains" won her praise from the anthologist Louis Untermeyer as an "unconscious imagist." Charles Olson's "fivers" in *The Maximus Poems,* in the sequences "Some Good News," "Stiffening in the Master Founder's Wills," and "Captain Christopher Levett (of York)," are in open form. The present "Thirty-nine Pentastichs" is a selection of recent short-line compositions in natural voice cadence, many of them marginal jottings and paraphrases of commonplace book notations.

THE TENDER LETTER

C'était à Paris. She was Jeanine, young, pretty and
bright. Une jeune fille bien élevée. They often had
me to Sunday dinner. I thought we were just friends.
Then the note to my hotel: "Je voudrais être ta
maîtresse" In three months she was dead of cancer.

I TRAVEL YOUR BODY

I travel your body, like the world,
your belly is a plaza full of sun,
your breasts two churches where blood
performs its own, parallel rites,
my glances cover you like ivy . . .

"I travel your body. . . . ": Octavio Paz, from Sunstone *(abridged),
translation by Eliot Weinberger.*

THE LIVING BRANCH

If I existed as a tree
I would not be a conifer, cone-bearing.
My nature would be deciduous, a long
Process of leaves, falling, falling
From the living branch.

Deborah Pease, the first stanza from a poem in The Feathered Wind.

ALL GOOD THINGS PASS

The girl at the order desk of the University
Press from whom I used to buy my Loeb Library
classics is now a telephone hitched to a
computer. She would wrap her long legs around
my neck and I imagined she was Tara of Cos.

THE SNAKE GAME

Henry looked like a shoeclerk but was a spell–
binder. He persuaded a friend to let him put a
garter snake into her vulva. Exciting at first
but then the snake wouldn't be pulled out. He
had to take her to the hospital emergency room.

Henry Miller.

THE LOCUST

Locust, beguiler of my loves and persuader of sleep,
mimic of nature's lyre, play for me a tune with your
talking wings to deliver me from the pains of care
and of love. In the morning I'll give you a fresh
green leek and drops of dew sprayed from my mouth.

Meleager of Gadara, fl. 60 B.C. *(condensed).*

THE IMMEASURABLE
BOUNDARIES

Heraclitus wrote that we would not discover
the boundaries of the soul even if we travelled
all the world's roads. At eighty I've traversed
a good many of them, but now I've stopped walking.
The boundaries of the soul are immeasurable.

THE HONEY BEE

You do everything, Melissa, just the
way your namesake the honey bee does.
When you're kissing me honey drips
from your lips, but when you ask
for money you have a sharp sting.

Marcus Argentarius (1st century A.D.*)*.

PENELOPE TO ULYSSES

Penelope to the tardy Ulysses:
do not answer these lines, but come, for
Troy is dead and the daughters of Greece
rejoice. But all of Troy and Priam himself
are not worth the price I've paid for victory.

Ovid, from the Heroides, *translated by Howard Isbell*.

THE LOVER'S COMPLAINT

I swear I do not ask too much of heaven:
O make that thoughtless girl
Who yesterday made me
Her spoils of war either love me
Or let me share her bed to prove I love her.

Ovid, a passage from the Ars Amatoria, *translation by Horace Gregory.*

THE FIRST TIME

It was the first time we had made love.
I asked her what she would like me to do
to give her pleasure. But she wouldn't
tell me. She said I must find out for
myself. It would be better so.

THE ANGLO-SAXON CHRONICLE

This year long dragons swam in fire
across the sky in Northumbria.
This was the year of the great gale.
And this year died Harthacanute:
Everything he did was unworthy of a king.

Guy Davenport, translator.

TANKA

In the *Dhammapada* it is written
that the body is a strong fortress
made up of bones, plastered with
flesh and blood, wherein lurk
pride, deceit, decay and death.

From the Dhammapada (*1st century* B.C.).

THE LONG FEET PEOPLE

Pliny relates in his *Natural History* that
in Iluria there's a race with feet a *pes*
long, turned backwards, with 16 toes. On
hot days they lie on their backs, using
their feet to shade themselves from the heat.

TWO FOR ONE

The painter Schiele knew he was two people,
and that he needed separate girls. When he
saw the Harms sisters in the street he hung
nude pictures of himself in his window. Edith
Harms married him. Adele became his model.

WORD SALAD

Neurologists call the babbling
of the patients in dementia "word
salad." Looking at recent verses
I realize that they are mostly
good examples of "word salad."

THE FANTASIST

Ronald Firbank the decadent novelist liked
to play out his fantasies. When Lady Cunard
invited him to lunch at the London Ritz he
studied the menu with care and ordered *one*
pea, which he sent back because it was cold.

THE PISSING OF THE TOADS

Concerning the venomous urine of toads, conceptions
are entertained which require consideration. That a
Toad pisseth, and this way diffuseth its venome,
is generally received, not only with us but also
in other parts, as the learned Scaliger observed.

From Thomas Browne's Pseudodoxia Epidemica, Enquiries into Cer-
tain Vulgar Errors (*1646*)

THE GOOD LIFE

Nabokov remembers that when he was young,
early in July his grandfather's carriage
and a team of horses would be loaded on a
railroad flatcar for the trip across Europe
to Biarritz in France for the annual holiday.

THE SEASHELL

Someone brought me a seashell.
Singing inside is a sea from a map.
My heart fills up with water
and little tiny fish, silvery, shadowy.
Someone brought me a seashell.

Federico García Lorca, translated by Alan S. Trueblood.

THE SMILE OF THE DESERT

In the desert I felt a thrill of pleasure—such as only
the captive delivered from his dungeon can experience.
The sunbeams warmed me into renewed life and vigour, the
air of the desert was a perfume, and the homely face of
Nature was as a smile of a dear old friend.

Sir Richard Burton, a passage from the Personal Narrative of a Pilgrimage
to Al-Madinah & Meccah (*1885*).

SALAD DRESSING AND
AN ARTICHOKE

It was please it was please carriage cup in an ice-
cream, in an ice cream it was too bended bended with
scissors and all this time. A whole is inside a part, a
part does go away, a whole is red leaf. No choice was
where there was and a second and a second.

Gertrude Stein, from Tender Buttons *(1914).*

THE SWEET SINGER

Sappho led a band of lovely girls
on Lesbos, and she sang to them
sweet singing: "Desire has shaken
my mind as wind in the mountain
forest roars through the trees."

THE LOVERS

Radha looked on the god Krishna who desired only
her, who long had wanted dalliance with her. His face
was possessed with desire. It showed his passion
through tremblings of glancing eyes. It was like
a lotus pond with a pair of wagtails at play.

An excerpt from the Sanskrit of Jayadeva's Gita-Govinda *(12th century*
A.D.*), the love songs of Krishna and Radha, translated by George*
Keyt.

THE WRITER AT WORK

On opening night of his play *Under Milk Wood*,
Dylan Thomas is backstage lying on his tummy
writing new lines for the cast: "Organ Morgan
at his bedroom window playing chords on the
sill for the fishwife gulls in Donkey Street."

THE GOD OF THE SUN AND FIRE

Glory to Agni, the high priest of the sacrifice.
We approach you, Agni, with reverential homage in
our thoughts, daily, both morning and evening.
You the radiant, the protector of sacrifices,
the constant illuminator, be as a father to us.

Excerpt from the First Mandala of the Rig Veda (circa *1500 B.C.*),
    abridged.

THE MAGIC FLUTE

That summer in Munich we were Papageno and Papagena.
We walked along the Isar and in the Englische Garten
and went to a different opera almost every night. But
it was Mozart who set us dreaming and made us fall
in love. Beautiful days and now happy memories.

THE RAVAGED VIRGIN

Aphrodisia in Anatolia is famed in mythic
history because it is recorded in Hesiod's
Theogony that there Zeus raped the nymph
Cleonia. He did it by disguising himself
as a water buffalo. She said it hurt a lot.

ODD GOINGS ON IN PHILADELPHIA

The painter Eakins was an odd duck. For him art
depended on the nude figure. But using nude
models wasn't enough. He wanted his girl students
to know the "joints and machinery" of the body.
He had himself photographed with them in the buff.

THE MAN OF TAO

The non-action of the wise man is not inaction.
It is not studied. It is not shaken by anything.
The sage is quiet because he is not moved,
Not because he wills to be quiet.
Still water is like glass.

A fragment from Thomas Merton's version of The Way of Chuang
Tzu *(1965).*

AN UNUSUAL GIRL

In Lucerne beautiful Birgita liked to circle
the Matterhorn in her Piper Cub. Evenings you
might find her with friends in her bathtub
enjoying live fish in an intimate way while
the phonograph played Schubert's *Trout Quintet*.

THE HETAERA

Ani Leasca, a Greek cocotte who worked Zurich,
could have modelled for Apelles. I never fingered
her expensive flesh, but when she wasn't engaged,
she liked to play pool in the Dolder, regaling
me with the kinks of the richest men in Europe.

THE RIGHT GIRL

Rufinus advised Thelon to beware a girl who seems
too eager. Or one who hangs back too long. One is
too quick, the other too slow. Look for one neither
too plump nor too thin. Too little flesh is as bad
as too much. Best, he said, never to run to excesses.

THE RESCUE

From New Orleans Tenn wrote me a wonderfully
comical letter. He was being relentlessly
pursued by a pretty girl. She was cramping
his style; would I get her off his back? A
very sexy girl; she soon had me on *my* back.

THE SCULPTOR

Brancusi didn't have much to say but he
cooked a great Romanian stew and liked
after eating to swing upside down by his
knees on a monkey's trapeze while his
phonograph blared out Ravel's *Bolero*.

GOOD PHILOSOPHY

When I give you an apple, if you love me
from your heart, exchange it for your
maidenhead. But if your feelings are what
I hope they are not, please take the apple
and reflect on how short-lived is beauty.

Plato (4th century B.C.).

AN EXQUISITE LIFE

Robert Montesquiou, the exquisite model
for Proust's Charlus, kept pet bats in
silver cages, and for his famous receptions
had each room of his dwelling sprayed
with a different suggestive perfume.

THE CRANE

Go away, crane! Leave the garden!
You have not told my love,
the prince of the seashore,
the torment that I suffer.
Go away, crane! Leave the garden!

Lines from the Tamil of the Shilappadikaram *(3rd century A.D.),
translated by Alain Daniélou.*

THE INVITATION TO MAKE LOVE

Show her drawings of animals making love, then
of humans. The sight of erotic creatures such
as geese will make her curious. Write amorous
messages to her on palm leaves. Tell her your
dreams about her. Tickle her toes with your finger.

Excerpts from the Sanskrit of Vatsyayana's Kama Sutra
(circa 5th century A.D.), translated by Alain Daniélou.

Two Segments from the Long-Poem-in-Progress

f r o m B Y W A Y S

The Rubble Railroad and *In Trivandrum*

A Note on the Metric

In composing the long autobiographical poem "By-ways," a work-in-progress of which the pages that follow are segments, I am intentionally avoiding rhetoric and verbal decoration. I would like to achieve a tone of colloquial speech and a pace for fast reading. Let's call "Byways" narrative verse. It is certainly not lyric poetry. A friend has called it a suitable receptacle for recollections. I owe the metric to my old friend and mentor the poet Kenneth Rexroth. He perfected the essentially three-beat line in his travel poem *The Dragon & The Unicorn*, which I published at New Directions in 1941.

It was October of 1945, only five
Months after the end of World War
Two. I was living in Paris, back
In my old digs in the rue du
Saint Père, trying to write a
Novel about life in Pittsburgh
In my youth, but the more I put
Down the worse it got. So I was
Glad when I had a letter from my
Old friend Herbert Blechsteiner
In Cologne saying that he had
Been able to wangle the use of
An Army car, with driver and
Gas ration, and would I like to
Join him for a week to inspect
What was left of Germany after
The bombing. Herbert, who was
Fluent in six languages, was
The greatest wangler I ever
Encountered. Anything he wanted
He would get, and at a bargain
Price. And he would do the
Same for his friends. This
Genius came from his years in
The Middle East. He had been
Born into a large family who
Were traders in antiquities.
There were branches of Blech-
Steiner Ltd. from Bombay to
Lisbon, all run by Herbert's
Uncles or cousins. London was

The province of Herbert's
Brother Ulrich, with a rather
Grand shop on Jermyn Street
Not far from the Cavendish
Hotel, where Rosa Lewis, one
Of the mistresses of Edward VII,
Still held sway. Herbert had
Served an apprenticeship at the
Shop in Damascus, where he
Picked up spoken Arabic, but
His heart was in languages and
Writing. He came back to Paris,
Where he lived with the uncle
There and did his time at the
Sorbonne in linguistics.

I took the Berlin Express but
Got off at Mannheim to board a
Steamer down the Rhine, this for
The sight of the Rhenish castles
Perched on the hilltops and
Vineyards cascading down to the
River. In Cologne I found a
Daimler-Benz sedan parked at
The Hotel Gruber. It had a
Little U.S. Army pennant on the
Front mudguard, so that would
Be Herbert. The driver, a sergeant,
Seeing my bag, leapt from the
Car to open the door and salute.
This saluting bit went on all
Through the trip. It embarrassed
Me because I'd managed with
Some effort to avoid the war.
"Can't you get him to stop the

Saluting?" I asked Herbert,
Who replied, "I told him you were
A bigshot in the OSS." I'd been
Wondering for some time why
Herbert stayed on with the Army
As only an interpreter. That
Evening at the Drei Hirschen
(Herbert would know the best
Place to eat in any city) over
A fine bottle of Gewürztraminer,
He explained that Germany was
Awash with displaced artworks.
Some were things that GI's had
Stolen. Others were things that
Starving owners who didn't have
Enough food cards for their
Families had to sell, often for
A song. Herbert's business was
To pick up such treasures and
Get them out to his relatives
In the Blechsteiner offices in
Army mail pouches which weren't
Censored. And how, I asked, did
He come by such an elegant auto?
Kindness of a Brigadier, he told me,
A charming fellow from New York
Who was a collector of etchings.
"I got him a prime Dürer, museum
Quality. He couldn't do enough
For me."

Next morning I accompanied Herbert
On his rounds. He needed some cash
And tackled a fat little dealer
Whose luxurious shop near the Dom

Betokened a sharpie set to catch
Tourists. Herbert was showing him
A superb Tibetan devil thanka he
Had picked up from one of the
Gurkhas in a British regiment that
Was stationed near Hanover. The
Dealer was no match for Herbert's
Salesmanship, which included verse
Quotations supposedly from the
Book of the Dead. Spotting me as
An American, Herr Plumps brought
Out a painting which he claimed
Was a Franz Marc, one of the
Blauer Reiter group, the man who
Did the famous bright red horses.
It was handsome, but Herbert
Pulled his ear to signal me that
It was a fake. And we left the shop.

Setting out for Frankfurt we
Stopped at the railroad station
To pick up the magnificent
Alexander who arrived from
Berlin to join up with us. I
Have selected the adjective
With care. Alexander Gruener,
Who had been Herbert's night
And day companion throughout
The war, was the embodiment
Of Hitler's prescription for
The ideal Teuton: nearly two
Meters tall, shoulders like
An ox but waist like a wasp;
Blue eyes, blond hair, and
A mien serious with determination;

His only shortcoming was that he
Was at heart a communist, which
Made him acceptable to Herbert as
A lover. The first few days we
Were together Alexander viewed
Me with suspicion, he couldn't
Quite place me in relation to
Herbert. Was I a rival? But he
Gradually got the picture that
We were just friends. He relaxed
And we got on well. His idea of
Amusements was to correct my
German and make the conventional
European's jokes about America.
He was soon calling me "der
Cowboy" and demonstrating his
Prowess in arm wrestling.

The bombing damage that we had
Seen in Cologne was slight; it
Had not been a primary target.
But Frankfurt was another story.
The center of the city had been
Flattened. Beautiful old quarters
Which I remembered from earlier
Visits were a desolation of
Destruction. The madness of war.
While we were in Germany I kept
A diary. When I got back to
Paris I put parts of it into verse:

> *In Frankfurt*
>
> Gray hungry men are loading
> debris from a blasted house

into the little dump cars of
the rubble railroad
                    this is
the line that makes its run
from death to hope
                        its tracks
are laid on blocks in every
German city & when one street
is cleaned they move them to
the next
            it pays no dividends
but runs all day and will for
7 years
            their shovels probing
hunger-slowly in the settled
wrack turn up a twisted, rust-
ing spoon. They all put down
their tools and pass it around
appraising worth or use
                            but
it's too bad they toss it in
the cart
            I pick it out and put
it in my pocket
                    I want that
spoon
            they stare I blush and
offer cigarettes they take &
thank and I walk off
                    I want
their spoon I'll take it home
back to the other world. I'll
need it there to learn to eat.
the men, and there were women
too in the work crews, were a
miserable looking group. They
were obviously undernourished,

dressed in rags, some of the
men in remnants of wehrmacht
uniforms, all of them so tired
they had to rest, leaning on
their shovels every few minutes.

How Did They Look?

The face narrows
the skin tightens on the cheekbones
the mouth & lips tighten
the cheeks suck in a bit
the eyes sink back into the skull
the eyes are dull seeming
the circles under the eyes deepen
and darken
the hair thins and grays
that's just the head
the body?
I couldn't bear to look.

Heading to Munich we couldn't
Go by the autobahn because it
Had only been rebuilt in sections.
Better to head south on small
Roads where we could enjoy the
Countryside, zigzagging from one
Rural road to another. It was
A welcome escape from the wreckage
Of the war. Pristine villages
Where the farming life was still
Going on. Hedgerows and poplar
Trees separating the meadows.
But there were few cows or sheep
In the meadows. They had been
Eaten. Where we stopped for

A lunch of kaiserschmarren in
An inn there was a small
Church beside the place, one
That had the slavic onion
Top on its spire. There a peasant
Wedding was taking place which
We watched for a half hour.
No cars about, there was so
Little gas. The bride and groom
Went off in a farm cart drawn
By a white horse so ancient he
Could hardly walk. We made a
Dip down to the Danube to see
The great gothic cathedral at
Ulm which had not been hurt.

In Munich we linked up with
An old friend of Herbert's,
The famous photographer Max
Faber. Max was touring around
Germany shooting the ruins for
The Air Force, which wanted a
Record of their handiwork for
The allied archives. He showed
Us his portfolio. Many of his
Shots were magnificent as art,
Giant sculptures in their way,
Especially where they dealt
With tall buildings that had
Only partially collapsed. The
Work depressed Max. In
His ebullient, gay way he was
A very jolly fellow, full of
German and macabre Jewish jokes
And stories. We spent a lot of

Time going around Munich with
Him. The sights of destroyed
Munich hurt me more than had
Frankfurt because I knew the
City well from the summer when
I had lived there, quartered with a
German family who were supposed
To teach me some German. I was
Only seventeen then, much more
Interested in the maedelis I
Picked up at the opera and in
The big English Garden Park.
Although the factories which
Were the targets for the air
Raids were outside the city
Proper, the aim of those who
Released the bombs was not
Good. Many of the cultural
Monuments were demolished.
Both of the pinakotheks had
Been hit, though fortunately
The paintings had been hidden
In saltmines and mountain
Caves. The buildings on both
Sides of the regal avenues,
The Maximilienstrasse and the
Ludwigstrasse, were smashed.
The Wittelsbach palaces were
Down, and in the business center
The Marienplatz and the rathaus
Town hall were in bad shape.

As we wandered about the city,
Where rubble railroads and
Their crews were working here

And there, we noticed another
Presence: large numbers of
American soldiers. They didn't
Seem to be doing anything except
Killing time. I talked to
A few of them to get a
Feel of how, as they waited
To be shipped home, they
Felt about their situation
As conquerors of an old
Culture. And about the
Desolation their planes
Had wrought. Their chief
Expressions were of boredom
And of anger that repatriation
Was taking so long. I tried
Later to get it down in a poem.

Song of the GI's and the MG's

We are the lords of the cigarette
    & the green passport
        we do the best we can
we rule the world unwillingly
    & have good intentions
        we do the best we can
we are most of us sorry that you
    are always so hungry
        we do the best we can
we are unaccustomed to governing
    & make some mistakes
        we do the best we can
we often marry your girls after we
    have seduced them
        we do the best we can

we are hurt when you resist our plans
            for your re-education
                        we do the best we can
            we will help you try to clean up
                        the bomb mess we made
                                    we do the best we can
            we are the lords of the cigarette
                        & the green passport
                                    we really do mean to do
                                    the best we can for you.

One evening Max invited us out to
His place in Schwabing, the artists'
Quarter out Ludwigstrasse beyond
The Siegestor. That is the quarter
Renowned for Oktoberfests, a week
Of merriment and carousing as famed
As our Mardi Gras in New Orleans.
There wouldn't be one that year,
Of course, but I hear now that it's
Going strong as ever again. Max's
Residence could hardly be called
An apartment. One side wall of
The building had been bombed off,
But Max had made a false wall
With canvas nailed onto salvaged
Posts. Electric power had not yet
Been restored but there were half a
Dozen candles. Max had an Army friend
And there was Jack Daniels from the
PX. He had assembled some artists
And several pretty girls. It was
An eventful party as this poem
Tells it, not a happy one for the girl.

Max's Party

One of our new aristocrats
the knights of the air en–
thralls (he thinks) a half–
starved German tart with his
exploits while he gets drunk
then he passes out poor girl
she has to hit the street again
without a meal the MP's
cart him off in their jeep.

And one of the artists
Had a tale to tell.

Hard to Translate

My friend Klaus a German goes
to the MG travel office for a
permit to visit Switzerland old
      friends in Berne

have invited him they will feed
and fatten him for three weeks and
clear some of the misery mist
      out of his brain

The MG official feels like a little
joke and kids Klaus "why ever
do you want a trip? you Germans
      should stay here

at home and enjoy your hunger–
strafe" (that word is rather hard
to translate as it means hunger–
      punishment but it

also suggests the strafing that
God was supposed to give to the
English) Klaus winces but keeps
    hold of his tem-

per he patiently tells the man
(who is a Jew) about his impris-
onment under the Nazis in the
    end he gets his

permit all right the man is a
good egg and meant to give it
to him all the time he was just
    feeling like his

little joke but he should not
have said that Klaus tells me
such things go to the bone and
    they stick there.

My happiest day in Munich was
When I took the little local train
South to Gauting, a village which is
Halfway to the Starnbergersee,
To visit the Heys, the family
With whom I had spent the summer
Years before to learn German.
Such nice people. I was sad
When I'd heard recently that
They were in terror of the Nazis.
They weren't Jews but the son,
Fritzi, had been expelled from
Munich University. The father
Who painted artwork for post-

Cards was in trouble because
He had declined to paint
The leader of a Nazi parade.

Every Saturday when I left them
I feared I might not see them again.
But when I called on the Heys
Now all seemed well. I walked out
To their house from the Gauting
Station and nothing was changed
Except that the watchdog Gunter
Had expired. Herr Hey was painting
Away in his attic studio. He
Had received a commission from
The Prinzregenten Theatre to do
Cards from scenes of Mozart's
Operas. They read me letters
From Fritz who had escaped
To India and was finishing
His engineering degree at the
University of Allahabad. And
There, my special blessing, was
Dear Frau Hey working in her
Beautiful flower garden. She
Was the one who was in charge
Of my German lessons. How I
Vexed her because I had
"Ungenügend anlegung"
For irregular verbs and things
That required memorization.
But she was gentle in her
Reproaches; she remembered
What it was like to be a
Student at seventeen. She
Imposed no penalties. I

Could take the train in to
Munich for the opera as often
As I wanted as long as I
Was back by midnight.

My best friend was my bicycle.
After lunch I'd take off on
It riding for miles through
The manicured paths of the
Towering forests. Peasants
Picked up every stick and
Carted them home on their
Little handcarts. "Grüss
Gott," I would shout to the
Gatherers as I pedalled
Past them, and "Grüss Gott
Herr" they would reply from
The shadowy depths of the
Forest. If it was a warm day
I would ride down to the top
Of the Starnbergersee, a
A big lake that runs nearly to the
Foot of the Alps. There was
A schwimmbad there where I'd
Change into my trunks and
Rent a bathchair in which I
Could stretch out to sun
Myself as I looked up at the
Mountains, the Alps above
Garmisch and Mittenwald
With the top of the mighty
Zugspitz peering over them.
One day I fell asleep in
The sun. When the old man
Who ran the schwimmbad woke

Me up I saw that I was the
Last. "You should have
Wakened me," I told him.
"No," he said, "I looked you
Over and could tell that
You were having a good
Dream. That's what all of us
In this country need now, a few
Good dreams."

Herbert and Alexander wanted
Me to drive up to Berlin with
Them but I'd had enough of
Ruins and suffering people.
I took the train from Munich
To Paris and tried to buckle
Down to work on my novel.
But it was hard to concentrate.
Pittsburgh suddenly seemed like
A place that never existed
In real life. What I had seen
In Germany kept flooding my
Brain. It was a long time, even
After I'd returned to the States,
Before I was able to put my
Heart in the book. One day as
I was avoiding work, this little
Poem appeared on my notebook
Page. It had written itself.

    O Frères Humains

    The rubble railroad
    carries freight
    that's more than loads

of stone and dirt
it carries off
an age's hate
and puts it with
a people's heart

the cars are dumped
beyond the city
and then come back
to load once more
o brother men
at last learn pity
return them full
with love to share.

In Trivandrum

My next stop in India that year
(Which was 1953, as best I can
Recall) was Trivandrum, a little
But lovely city in the region now
Known as Kerala, which was in
Colonial times a princely state
Ruled by the Portuguese, then
The Dutch, and then the English,
Who called it Cochin. Vasco de
Gama landed his ships at
Cochin in 1502, reckoning it the
Finest port on the Arabian Sea
South of Bombay. Cochin has a
Heavy rainfall, making the land
Rich for rice, tapioca, pepper and
Vegetables. The landscape is set
With graceful coconut palms and
Many ponds and little ornamental
Waterways. The language mainly
Is Malayalam, but Trivandrum
Holds also a settlement of Jews
That boasts the oldest synagogue
In Asia. Christians of differing
Sects are scattered all over the
Subcontinent. Many myths tell
Of the coming of Christianity
To India. In Malabar they think
The Apostle Thomas ("doubting
Thomas") arrived in Cochin in
A.D. 52 to take up the work of
Conversion. But on the eastern

Coast people tell you Thomas
Built his church in Madras on
A hill known as The Mount.

I had come to Trivandrum to
Meet the novelist Raja Rao.
Along with R. K. Narayan of
Mysore, Raja Rao was, in those
Days and probably still is, the best
Indian writer working in English.
(How good the native writers
May be, since they compose in
thirteen major languages, is
Hard to guess. Few of them can
Read the works of the others.)
But I had read Raja Rao's novel
The Serpent and the Rope and I
Had no doubt in my mind that
He was first class. I had heard
Rumors that he had finished
A new novel. I wanted to find
Him. The rumors were true.
After we had been together for
Two days, during which Raja
Had assessed my enthusiasm
For Indian life and culture, he
Placed the manuscript of his
New book, *Kanthapura,*in my
Hands, saying: "I think you'll
Like this. My friend Mr. Forster
Has been over it and says it's
A good book about India as
She is today, after Gandhi."
I didn't need Forster's praise to
Convince me that this was a

Masterpiece. *Kanthapura* is
A book like no other I'd read,
A magical book that brings the
Spell of India to the western
Reader. New Directions brought
The book out at once, and after
Many reprintings it remains
As fresh and compelling as it
Was when I first encountered it.

"Kanthapura" is a typical small
Village of southern India in
Which the changing life of all
Castes, impacted by Gandhi's
Revolution of independence
From the British, is the main
Force. Young Moorthy back
From the city with "new ideas,"
Works to break down the old
Barriers. Nonviolence, as
Gandhi taught it, is his way
Of mobilizing the villagers to
Action. But his efforts are met
With violence from the police
And the rich landowners. The
Remarkable thing in the book
To me is its colloquial manner.
Rao's narrator is an old woman
Of the village who is imbued
With the legendary history of
Her region, the old traditions
Of Hinduism and the Vedic
Myths. She knows the past.
The stories of the villagers,
And her commentary on her

Neighbors is both pungent and
Wise. In her speech are echoes
Of the traditional folk-epics
Such as the *Ramayana*. But
How does Rao manage this
When writing in plain lucid
English? He has somehow
Made us hear native speech
In his narrator's extraordinary
Anglo-Indian language. He
Has a fine ear. He had known
The intonations and rhythms
Of the villagers as a child when
He was growing up in Mysore.
Then, because he came from
A prominent family, he had
Opportunities unusual for
An Indian, the University of
Madras and study in France at
Montpelier and the Sorbonne.

Traipsing about the countryside
With Raja as my guide was a
Great pleasure. The land is so
Verdant, and the busy life of
The inland waterways delighted
Me, the small open ferryboats,
Mostly motorized but now and
Then a boat with the red lateen
Sails of the ancient Arab dhows
That had first opened up the
Malabar coast. Raja had no
Car, but we borrowed bicycles
With which we followed the
Footpaths or the rough roads

Created by old bullock carts
Whose once-round wheels
Had been worn squarish by
Long use. We saw the villagers
Ploughing with their cattle,
Humped slaves who would work
Every day until they dropped,
Sleeping nights out in the rain.

Yet these cows seemed to live
A happier life than the sacred
Cows you find in Calcutta who
Live in the streets, sleep on the
Sidewalks and are fed by the
Faithful—once I was watching
As children gave candy bars
To a Calcutta cow—all this
Because the people believe
That cattle are descended, at
Least symbolically, from those
The Gopis watched over for
Lord Krishna at Brindaban.
We saw sheep and chickens
Around the hutments but no
Pigs. Little monkeys aplenty in
The coconut palms. The men
Distill a palm wine which they
Call "toddy." We were offered
Cups of it which tasted so awful
I could scarcely get mine down
Out of politeness. It looked like
Rotten eggs. But the intoxicating
Effect is said to be considerable.
Knowing Malayalam, Raja Rao
Was able to converse with the

People, who were not shy. They
Gathered around us to talk and
Raja interpreted for me. He said
They had never seen anyone
As tall as I (I'm six foot five).
They wanted to know where I
Came from and what I ate to
Get so big. Did I practice yoga?
Or some other occult mastery?

Some of them invited us into
Their thatched huts to show
Us with pride the rice-paste
Abstract paintings on their
Walls and thresholds. Raja
Taught me on that visit to
Eat curry and other Indian
Foods with my fingers, for no
Brahmin would ask for utensils.
It would be a breach of the rules
Of caste. But don't ask me to
Show you how it's done; I was
A poor pupil. The weather was
Hot in Cochin, of course, all
That moisture with the sun
Smoldering down through it.
Raja loaned me a dhoti, much
Better than my European pants
And shirt. But I managed more
Than once to get the skirt of
My dhoti caught in my bicycle
Chain, with resultant tumbles.
Our audience was amused. In
The evenings we had our curry
At Raja's home, which was for

Me a further trial of the fingers
In place of a fork. His was an
Extended family living in a
Small house in Trivandrum
And to this day I'm not sure
Who was who. Many women
In their saris smiled at me and
Said nothing. Only the men
Joined us at table. The women
Ate apart, maybe in the kitchen
Which I was not shown. Then
Raja and I went out to wander
The streets of the old town with
Its Dutch-style buildings. Parts
Of it could have been Delft or
Nijmegen. No street lights, not
Much light from the house
Windows; it was eerie. Bare
Feet in the darkness making
No noise. It was enchanting too.

We went to a show by
A troupe of Kathakali dancers
—Very exciting. Most of the
Dancing in South India, such
As the gliding style of Bharata
Natya, is tranquil, except for
An accompaniment of soft
Drumming; movement is
By the arms and hands, and
The "story" is told in classic
Mudras that have assigned
Meanings. Kathakali however
Is the opposite, violent motion
Most of the time. In a way it

Reminded me of the dramatic
Posturing in Japanese Kabuki.
For the westerner one of the
Attractions of Kathakali is
The costumes. Also the masks
Of the male dancers, sculpted
And grotesque. Vivid primary
Colors. Faces to scare children.
Demons and heroes. Men as
Tigers, as serpents. Terrifying.
Much magic, much death.

The plays are given outdoors
And always at night, often not
Finishing until the dawn. In
Darkness the great brass lamps
Flicker and add to the mystery.
The audience sits on the ground
(Though Raja Rao and I were
Honored with chairs). Men,
Women and children usually
Are separated. Two drummers,
Sounding their drums with
Their hands, often in very fast
Rhythms, provide the music.
The actors speak passages of
Verse that narrate the action
Of the play. The dialogue is
Sung by two singers who stand
At the back of the "stage." Now
The stories of the plays are told
In Malayalam rather than the
Classic Sanskrit, but they are
Still the ancient texts, epics like
The *Ramayana* (which reports

The heroic adventures of Rama
When he rescues his wife from
The demon-king Ravana of
Ceylon) or the *Mahabharata*
(Which recounts the endless
Struggle between two families,
The Pandavas and Kauravas,
Though the pre-eminent hero
Of the poem is the god Krishna)
Or the *Gita Govinda* (a cycle of
Poems about Krishna). These
Are traditional tales known
Almost universally in India
To all classes, just as Greek
Myths and Bible stories
Are known to us in the West.
In origin they go back perhaps
A dozen thousand years to
The oral tradition of village
Storytellers, the entertainers
Of that culture, just as our
Homeric epics are thought
To have been composed and
Revised and embellished by
Generations of warrior poets
Who recited them around the
Smoky campfires of ancient
Armies. At some point these
Original Hindu poems were
Transcribed into Sanskrit by
The pandits and gurus. Then
The final step was translation
Into the various vernaculars,
Hindi, Urdu, Tamil, Marathi,
Malayalam, and many others.

The evening of Kathakali was
Dramatic and thrilling though
Very long: it went on way past
Midnight. Raja Rao briefed me
On the unfolding motifs and
Action as the play progressed.
Then the next day at dusk we
Experienced something even
More remarkable. Through Rao
I had met Professor Vivekananda
Who taught in the college at
Ernakulam on the coast north
Of Trivandrum. Vivekananda
Knew Sri Nalanda, a Vedantist
Guru from Bombay who was
Visiting friends in a small
Village in the Cardamon
Hills. It was a rough trip
Getting there in a jitney
But we made it and the sage
Welcomed us cordially to one
Of the most intense occasions
Of my visit. I wouldn't have
Believed the background story
Vivekananda told me about Sri
Nalanda if we had been in any
Country but India, where the
Occurrence of wonders is so
Continual and many minds
Are saturated with the occult.
Gurus, holy men, sadhus, yogis.
Sannyasis all over the place,
Some with begging bowls, or
Smeared with ashes, or naked
In the streets. Being holy, being

A devotee of this god or that,
Depending on hand-outs from
The public, is a way of life.

I was told by Vivekananda that
Nalanda came from a favored
Middle-class family. He had
Done well at school and had
Entered the railway service,
Where he had also done well,
Ending up as superintendent
At Bangalore. A faultless
Reputation, a married family
Man; no hint of any instability.
But his whole life was changed
When one night, while taking
A walk in the countryside, he
Met with a celestial messenger.
He knew by the godlike
Aura radiating around the
Old man's head that this
Stranger by the roadside was
Heaven-sent. The ancient
Invited Nalanda to sit on the
Edge of a ditch and said that he
Had flown from Dharamsala
In the Himalayas to instruct
Nalanda, who indeed believed
It because like all Indians he
Believed in parakinesis. He
Knew that servants of the gods,
Like the apsarases, could move
Themselves over thousands of
Miles in the blink of an eye.

They talked together all night.
Then at dawn the messenger
Vanished, but not until he had
Laid on Nalanda the solemn
Injunction to make himself
A serious teacher of Vedanta.
Nalanda was careful to keep
What had happened a secret,
But immediately he began to
Study Vedanta with the wise
Men of the region, giving up
His worldy aspirations, and
He undertook long hours of
Meditation. In a few years he
Was renowned as an adept in
The doctrines of Vedanta and
Their significance, and also as
An eloquent elucidator of the
Ultimate meaning of reality,
Which, as it descends from the
Ancient Vedic texts such as the
Upanishads, concerns especially
The state of being beyond good
And evil, existence beyond and
Above mere knowledge. Then
Sri Nalanda was ready to begin
His teaching, and soon many
Devotees were attracted to him.

On the night of my visit to him
With Professor Vivekananda
The setting for Sri Nalanda's
Lecture was not unlike that of
The Kathakali. It was outdoors

But a tarpaulin extended over
The bathchair in which the sage
Reclined as he talked. He was a
Small man whose somewhat
Birdlike features were belied
By a deep, almost hoarse voice,
More military than priestly.
His head was bald and glinted
As if astrally in the flaring light
Of the brass lanterns. He had
Piercing black eyes. He wore a
White dhoti and sandals. The
Professor and I were seated on
Chairs near him but the others,
The devotees, sat on the ground
In a circle extending out into
The eerie dark. I felt that some
Kind of emanation was coming
From Nalanda into my own
Body, and I'd never had such
An experience before. It was
Not an unpleasant feeling. It
Was more like being a little
High on wine. I couldn't, of
Course, understand what he
Was saying, but Vivekananda
Whispered a word now and then.

I could see I was entirely out of
My depth. I'd had a course or
Two in philosophy at Harvard,
But the abstractions proposed
By Nalanda were from another
Thought-system, one for which
I was ill prepared. I caught bits

Of epistemology, whiffs of the
Philosophy of *Existenz,* but the
Frame was all alien. A different
Kind of mind, a sledgehammer
Of a mind, was at work. I gave
Up trying to understand and let
Myself drift as I watched, lost
In his gestures and intonations.

He lectured for about an hour,
Then rose to give his audience
The namatse blessing, with
Palms together, bowing in a
Circle to include everyone at
The gathering. Then came the
Gifts of food—bread, fruit, and
Vegetables laid out at his feet.
Nalanda asked Vivekananda
And me to stay on. The accent
Of his English was difficult, but
He was cordial, calling me "Mr.
Young America" with a warm
Smile. Vivekananda was well
Versed in Vedanta; they talked
For a half-hour in Malayalam;
And when it was time for us to
Go, Nalanda asked me if I had
A question. But my mind went
Blank: what could I ask of the
Great sage? He smiled and said:
"So, let *me* ask *you* a question.
In America, tell me, what do
They teach you is between two
Thoughts?" I could think of no
Answer to that. I had no answer.

"No matter," said Nalanda. "In
Time you may be ready for such
A question. But fix it in your
Mind. Do not forget it before
You are ready." And all these
Years I've remembered, though
I know I can never answer the
Question. I scarcely understand
It. And is Sri Nalanda still alive?
Wherever he may be, what is
The space between his thoughts?

On my last evening with Raja
Rao we cycled out to the beach
To watch the sunset—a good
One, the sky blazing with many
Colors. At first the setting sun
Seemed a small, distant disk,
But as darkness fell it grew and
Grew into a huge ball of fiery
Red. "That is the great god
Agni," Raja Rao told me, "the
Eternal fire. He is many things.
He is the most important of
The Vedic divinities. First, he
Is the god of the altar fire and
Its sacrifices. Then he is the
Mediator between gods and
Men. And beyond that he is the
God of lightning and the sun."

As we pedaled back through
The dark countryside toward
Trivandrum, we began to smell
The loveliest natural perfume

I've encountered anywhere in
Any country. It's the evening
Scent of India. The people in
Their huts are cooking their
Last meal of the day, using
Cow patties to fuel their fires.
Every patty the cows let fall
Is picked up and saved by the
Children. The smoke rises in
The warm night air softly. It's
A pungent smell and a little
Sweet. It's the smell of India,
Primeval India of the first
Gods and the first real people.

[*The author expresses his thanks to Hayden Carruth for
his editorial collaboration on "Trivandrum."*]

INDEX OF TITLES
AND FIRST LINES